HIV Stories

HIV Stories

The Archaeology of AIDS Writing
in France, 1985–1988

Jean-Pierre Boulé

Liverpool University Press

For Zoé

First published 2002

Liverpool University Press
4 Cambridge Street
Liverpool, L69 7ZU

British Library Cataloguing-in-Publication Data

ISBN 0-85323-568-6 cased
       0-85323-578-3 paper

Set in Caslon by
Koinonia, Manchester
Printed in the European Union by
Bookcraft Ltd, Midsomer Norton, Wilts

Contents

Acknowledgements

I should like to thank Robin Bloxsidge (my publisher), Andrew Kirk (editor), Richard Johnson, Murray Pratt and Mireille Rosello for their support, and the Faculty of Humanities at Nottingham Trent for granting me sabbatical leave for one semester in order to work on this project; the Inathèque de France (Paris) where I was able to view the television programmes featuring Aron and Simonin and the CRIPS (Paris) for allowing me to view the programme about Dreuilhe. For the chapter on Simonin, John Fletcher did his usual great translation job, and *French Cultural Studies* gave me permission to use an earlier version which had appeared as 'Michel Simonin: Le témoin oublié' in the special issue on 'AIDS in France', Vol. 9, Part 3, No. 27 (October 1998), which I co-edited. Ross Chambers commented on the manuscript, and I am very grateful for his generosity and for his belief in what I was doing; as well as his suggestion about the structure of the book, some of his own comments have been incorporated into the analysis. Davis Caron kindly allowed me to read his forthcoming book *AIDS in French Culture: Social Ills, Literary Cures* (University of Wisconsin Press, 2001). Finally, I was companioned in the writing of this book by my friend David Jackson, and we worked together right from the beginning. For both of us, it was a breakthrough not to work in isolation but co-operatively, letting someone else in at the stage of hesitant fumbling rather than to view the fetishised end product. Though the book is mine, many of the original readings of the texts were discussed with him and bear his imprint.

Needless to say, I am solely responsible for any shortcomings or inconsistencies the text may still contain.

Je voulais témoigner. Ça me paraissait une exigence intérieure.

I wanted to be a witness. It seemed to me to be an internal demand.

Jean-Paul Aron on being questioned about why he gave the interview 'Mon sida' ('My AIDS')

Introduction

This book offers an archaeology of AIDS writing in France from 1985 to 1988. The main focus is on the moment of the irruption into discourse of AIDS writing. I want to look at two aspects of this moment: the problem of how to write about a new and taboo topic, and the problem of the frameworks of discourse that are produced/reproduced in such writing, particularly the difficulty of breaking out of certain constraints. As an archaeological enterprise, my book disinters a body of writing about AIDS that appeared in France between 1985 and 1988 from the cultural oblivion to which most of the texts have been consigned. The six texts under consideration are written in the first person singular. They have various labels: 'real life/true story' ('histoire vécue'), diary, testimony, interview, confession, autobiography; at the outset, they could all be said to be 'autobiographical narratives' of some sort. Another common denominator is that none of them was presented as a 'novel'.[1] This book is a study of AIDS *writing* as opposed to a study of AIDS *novels*. I have used the term 'archaeology' in the title, a term associated with Foucault's method, but I would not claim that my reading is strictly Foucauldian, notably because of my psycho-social approach. I am aiming to write a history of the past by excavating meanings and practices around AIDS texts during the period in question, and by bringing to light what has been covered up, since almost no critical attention has been paid to the first writers in the AIDS field.[2] Hence my reading has elements of archaeology (trying to uncover buried statements from discourses) but also of genealogy, since I am looking at power and knowledge relations.

The specific virtue of addressing early AIDS writing is discovering how and why the authors invested in a particular genre, and how their voices go from being ignored, to being muffled, to being heard, before finally being eternally silenced (hence the study of genre is itself part of the struggle to find a voice or a form). Some startling facts emerge about the earliest AIDS writings in France. These were not, as was the case in other countries and with subsequent writing in France, predominantly gay. Apart from Dreuilhe and Aron, who had already been published, the other authors, as far as I am able to tell given the problem of pseudonyms, were totally unknown. As Chambers has said, it is the case internationally that middle-class, white, gay males were the only group sufficiently empowered to be able to write and publish at the beginning of the pandemic.[3] Murphy makes the point that gay men, either as writers or as subjects, dominate the written word on this particular subject.[4] So it is quite remarkable that of the texts under study here, only Dreuilhe, Simonin and Aron fit into this category, and that there are two presumed female authors and a heterosexual one. In the early years of the pandemic, the virus was mostly associated with gay men, so it is all the more remarkable that they do not dominate this corpus. This phenomenon may have a lot to do with constructions of nationality/sexuality relationships in the French context, with the discourse of heterosexual sexualities dominating others: issues of gender and heterosexual masculinities and femininities, especially the model of the nuclear family, are being defensively shored up at a moment of perceived vulnerability and openness to deconstruction. The liberalisation of sexualities in the 1960s and 1970s had created a threat to these traditional sexualities; hence they in turn found the power (and the need) to reassert their hegemony.

The question of the gender and sexual orientation of these writers is also linked to the French response to the AIDS crisis, and the fact that there was no gay community to speak of in France, nor any tradition of identity politics. There was indeed a resistance to any conception of homosexual identity or visibility, notably from Michel Foucault. Hence this created an extra barrier to writing a book about AIDS. As with the example of Aron, writing or speaking about AIDS was a double-disclosure of one's homosexuality and of one's serological status.[5] Of the six texts under study, three of the authors can be formally identified: Michel Simonin, Alain Emmanuel Dreuilhe and Jean-Paul Aron. According to Michel Danthe, who made enquiries with the respective publishers, the remaining three books were all written under pseudonyms: Hélène Laygues, Juliette and Mike Winer.[6] We are told that all names have been changed in the three books. In addition, Winer also changes geographical location, going as far as to have his book published in France and translated into French, although his story is set in the United States, so that people still living cannot be traced.

It is not my intention in any of the texts under consideration to take the textual narrator as being unproblematically the voice of the real author. As Barthes writes, '[…] *I* is nothing other than the instance saying *I*.[7] I am aware of poststructuralist debates around the notion of an 'author', best encapsulated by the work of Foucault and Barthes.[8] As feminist poststructuralists write, 'The subject of discourse, author or speaker, is itself caught in [a] web of calculations. Truth is at once a material, discursive, political and subjective question.'[9] As Chambers demonstrates, the type of writing under study here is more 'oriented to the open-endedness of witness than to memory'.[10] Furthermore, as Freeman writes, '[…] the process of rewriting the self cannot help but culminate in fictions, in selective and imaginative literary constructions of who we have been and are […]'.[11] I deal later with the binary truth/fiction. But the fact of the matter is that I must adhere to the evidence available in the texts. In the absence of any archives containing reviews of the books from the time of publication, despite repeated approaches to the publishers, the only available evidence is the text.

One of the most significant aspects of early AIDS writing is that very often only the story survives, and it tells the death of the author.[12] Of all the authors studied, as far as I know, only Hélène Laygues has survived since she is described as HIV-negative, although her book still deals in great detail with Martin's agony and subsequent death. Aron, Dreuilhe and Simonin all died; Juliette does not appear to have very long left by the end of the book, and Winer's death is announced in his text. As Chambers puts it, readers of AIDS texts are made to face 'the fact of the author's death', and are positioned as survivors, elaborating further on the notion of survivor's guilt.[13]

Early AIDS writing adopted a wide range of strategies in trying to get a hearing; yet these courageous attempts ran against a wall of fear and indifference, presumably grounded in a denial of AIDS itself, or at the very least an identification of AIDS as an American disease (and I use 'disease' advisedly here), invading France. The fears unmasked by these writings were dealt with by a denigration of their lack of professional accomplishment: their amateur status, their sometimes unliterary (unpolished, unsophisticated) approach to writing, their apparent belief that telling their story was the only thing needed to get a hearing (characteristics that today make it so interesting to read these writers). Hence they were ignored. When I was talking to a friend of mine about this project, he asked me if the books had any merit as 'literature'. I think that the question in itself should give rise to suspicion. In the liberal-humanist discourse, literature worthy of the name lies in the universal meaning expressed, the 'truth' about human nature being revealed by the text. Rightly, poststructuralists would claim that no such thing exists. In addition, the term *literature* tends to reflect dominant patriarchal discourse. Other discourses are subordinated by being called *writings*, as in women's writings, or black women's writings. These have had to be satisfied with the margins of literature and literary departments in universities, until their recognition via the cultural studies route. So my project is also a political one in as much as I want to break with traditional versions of subjectivity, knowledge and power.

In many ways, none of these books (with the exception of Dreuilhe's

Corps à corps) could have existed as 'novels' or 'literature' because their form is driven by the pressure of the subject-matter and the urgency of their authors' desire to draw attention to it. They become visible as an infringement of literature, in the margins of literature. What is now covered up, and what I am unearthing, is that for a short period in France there was a real attempt to democratise cultural expression and to render it accessible to people normally excluded, in a form not usually identifiable with what is called 'literature'. This in turn acknowledges the policing of the categories 'literature' and 'writing' in France. These people succeeded in getting published against the overwhelming opposition of the sanctity of French literature and all its establishments, from *grandes écoles* to the *Académie française*. Another way of looking at this would be to say that it is precisely because these works were not presented as *novels* that they were allowed to be published. The dominant discourse in France did not feel threatened, since from the moment of their existence they were marginalised as 'writings'. Hence, allowing their publication would not be an attempt at democratisation but a further controlling device for the ruling hegemonic discourse.

In the history of AIDS writing in France, the breakthrough was made suddenly in the early 1990s with Hervé Guibert's *À l'ami qui ne m'a pas sauvé la vie*, which enjoyed great commercial success,[14] and Cyril Collard's film *Les Nuits fauves*.[15] These two authors themselves found their literary voice as a result of writing about AIDS. AIDS became a received *topos* on the literary scene. The writing of these authors is also in the first person and it frequently takes the form of a fictionalising of autobiographical events and experiences. It makes sense to see the earlier first-person writing under study here, whether novelistic or testimonial, as precursive of these later works (though there are significant differences in the degree of fictionalisation of autobiographical elements). Marsan writes that in 1990 polemical, informative, medical and testimonial accounts were progressively being abandoned in favour of the 'AIDS-novel'.[16] But by the time Guibert's book was published, the authors under study had already contributed towards creating a receptive audience. Five years had elapsed between the first text and Guibert's novel; it takes time and struggle for a new topic to acquire its appropriate forms of representation and rhetoric. A sense of a genre slowly builds up, and the early books create readers' patterns of expectations. The more sophisticated writing of Bourdin, Guibert and De Duve can benefit from the trials and errors of the early writing which was trying to present something previously unknown and understood to be either ignored or mis-recognised; the later writers can avoid the genres which, with hindsight, only served to perpetuate the dominant discourse of oppression, and learn from the backlash suffered by some of the earlier writers after their work was published.[17] By 1990, AIDS had lost a lot of the stigma attached to it, and most people knew that everyone was potentially at risk (though not equally so), rather than only specific (misnamed) 'high-risk groups'. This has an impact on identification processes and readership. Over the last decade, AIDS writing has progressively become an established genre, branching out into sub-categories such as 'sida-roman' ('AIDS novel'), a term coined in France in 1991,[18] and 'sida-fiction'.[19] The first essays to be published on the subject have mostly focused on 'canonical' male writers, or those perceived as 'canonical' writers, usually at the expense of female writers,[20] or else have concentrated on giving an overview of the literature.[21]

By the early 1990s, the courageous precursors had ceased to exist. Apart from Dreuilhe's book and Aron's interview, the works are out of print, so the process of eternal silencing is already well under way. The fact that these texts were not heard at first is compounded by the fact that later texts have been very successful. At a moment when they could have been heard because the genre was being discovered by a larger public (from 1990 onwards), they were silenced a second time by the success of newer texts displacing them and rendering them obsolete. This is why, just over fifteen years after the first of these texts was published, my excursion into archaeology is necessary. These books would not find a publisher nowadays in France. The literary scene is extremely guarded. For instance, the now established discipline of gay and lesbian studies in the United Kingdom, North America and Australia is still looked upon with suspicion by French academics and does not break through into the mainstream,[22] except where it is transformed beyond recognition to fit in with French literary heritage. This is linked to France's tradition of Republicanism which will be explored later on in this introduction.

The reading of each text is based on a psycho-social approach, fitting into the broad category of sexual and gender politics. The study of each text is a blending of textual commentary, psychoanalytic theory and general social/cultural comment. My own theoretical position resembles a version of feminist poststructuralism but the emphasis is on giving attention to subject-positions and modes of *masculinity*. Feminist poststructuralism believes that 'the politics of theory, personal politics and the politics of social change are inextricably entwined'[23] and it is concerned with social change.[24] Different theoretical writers are used for each book studied. The basic framework I adopt is to look at these texts as sites of cultural practice, in order to trace how, in the mid-1980s, sets of discourses, social and individual identities, and material and social practices are organised around sexuality and gender politics, with specific emphasis on the dominant discourse of heterosexual masculinity which silences PWAs (persons with AIDS). By 'discourse' I mean a set of signifying practices and values which break down into different categories, for example, dominant or subordinated discourses. There are of course many different versions of heterosexual masculinities, and the dominant form which I have in mind is 'hierarchic heterosexuality' which, as defined by Hearn, is 'premised on an inequality of power between men and women. To develop egalitarian heterosexuality would necessarily mean a loss of domination of heterosexuality over other sexualities. In other words, heterosexuality that is not hierarchic undermines heterosexuality.'[25] Brittan, taking up Hearn's definition, explains that another target group of hierarchic heterosexuality is 'homosexuality', constantly denied access to institutional influence and authority so that the former remains the dominant discourse.[26] When I use the term masculinity, I include *heterosexual* and *homosexual* dimensions because, as Kimmel and Levine put it, 'Since there is no anticipatory socialization for homosexuality, boys in our culture all learn norms for heterosexual masculinity. This means that, gay or straight, men in our culture are cognitively oriented to think and behave sexually through the prism of gender.'[27] I shall not be dealing exhaustively with *all* discourses on AIDS in France since this would widen my project beyond the scope of the present line of enquiry.[28]

This book is chronological, within the two different parts, because the analysis goes hand in hand with the socio-political context of the time. It is therefore important to situate the texts under study within the period 1985–88. In doing so, it is worth bearing in mind the delays that led up to publication. The first book under consideration, *Sida, Témoignage sur la vie et la mort de Martin*, published in October 1985, is likely to have been written in 1984, if not earlier. It appears that Martin died in 1983 or 1984, and the flashback narrative goes right back to the period 1980–82. The last book, *Bienvenue dans le monde du sida!*, was published in January 1988, the printing being completed in December 1987, but we know from the narrative that the events take place in 1986. There might be a question as to why Mike Winer's book is included since it is supposedly set in the United States. The fact is that it was published in France and in the French language. It is therefore part of AIDS writing in France for the period 1985–88. Overall, if we take into account publishing delays, the period under study is the early eighties up to 1987.

There are various accounts of the AIDS pandemic, and I shall make use of Jeffrey Weeks's writings. The *New York Times* broke the story on 3 July 1981 with the headline 'Rare cancer seen in 41 homosexuals'.[29] Karposi's Sarcoma quickly became known as the 'gay cancer',[30] and when AIDS became the term generally accepted in 1982, it was often referred to as the 'gay plague'. By mid-1983, a general panic was under way, not only in the USA but elsewhere. Weeks distinguishes three distinct periods. 1981-83 saw a slowly increasing awareness of the crisis; 1983-86 was a period of moral panic with AIDS seen as a disease of 'the marginal and the promiscuous'.[31] There were innocent victims (people who had had blood transfusions), and guilty ones (gay men, drug addicts and prostitutes). By 1986, the various governments had realised that they needed to start managing the crisis, which was now widely recognised to be affecting the hetero-sexual population too. As I have said, the texts under study all fall within the first two periods of the pandemic, since the events of even the last one to be published took place in 1986. The other factor which will be illustrated in the various texts is that AIDS was seen primarily in France as 'a pure invention of American puritanism',[32] and this had a knock-on effect for prevention work before this myth was exploded in 1986; AIDS became 'a new plague brought from America'.[33]

Weeks's categorisation applies to the French situation, except that the first prevention campaign aimed at the general public took place only in January 1987, together with the passing of a bill authorising the advertisement of condoms.[34] A brief overview of France is now necessary in order to set the scene and afford points of comparison. ACT-UP Paris usefully points to the time span from July 1984 to March 1986 as a crucial time when, under Edmond Hervé as Health Minister, France remained totally apathetic.[35] The contaminated blood scandal took place during this period. It was also at this time that the American AIDS test (Abbott) came on to the market, and the French government delayed its approval in France for months in order to market the French test (Elisa) instead; a multi-million franc market was at stake. There then followed the dithering of La Sécurité sociale (the French health service) in deciding whether to pay for the test or not; this obviously had important implications for affordability. The test became available in France in 1985. In terms of public opinion regarding the pandemic, the French-owned television station Antenne 2 could still entitle a programme 'Le sida ou la peste du XXème siècle' ('AIDS or the Twentieth-Century Plague') on 4 March 1986; Marsan quotes an opinion poll following a television programme on 9 September 1988 in which 87 per cent of people were in favour of mass screening (though not compulsory screening).[36] And inevitably, the extreme right wanted to have 'sidatoria'[37] where HIV-positive people would be contained. The first prevention campaign *for gay men*, sub-sidised by the government, was launched at the end of 1988 in *Gai Pied*.[38] It seems that in France the moral panic, as described by Weeks, lasted well into 1988 and this will be analysed later. In 1988, three new bodies were created by the government: ANRS (Agence nationale de la recherche scientifique), AFLS (Agence française de la lutte contre le sida) and CNS (Conseil national sur le sida) under the aegis of the DGS (Direction générale de la santé). As Agar puts it, this was a step in the right direction, 'albeit a latterday response on the part of the government'.[39]

What seems to be apparent is that the various narrative strategies in the texts under study are related to the different social circumstances of the authors. Hence, for instance, the thriller genre favoured by Winer and to some degree by Juliette is connected to the period of moral panic in France (1983–88), and perhaps captures best the mood of the time. Another dimension is that there is enough fictionalising in both texts for readers not to be overtaken by moral panic as might happen with a more conventional autobiography or a diary; readers can always distance themselves by believing that it is only fiction. Simonin has nothing left to lose by the time he publishes his autobiographical narrative under his real name with his photograph on the front cover; he has already suffered every possible and imaginable discrimination, and appeared on television. Dreuilhe occupies a subject-position in the French intelligentsia that enables him to choose the 'journal' mode and to have his book published by Gallimard as well as translated and subsequently published in America, though this does not take anything away from his bravery. In each of the texts under study, there is a fine balance between distancing/secrecy and 'truth'. The act of writing about this subject-matter is itself, by the reflexive nature of writing, a way of coming to terms with internal chaos and of self-(re)integration. Aron, by choosing to speak in an interview, does not even allow himself the possibility of fictional voices, and he repeats the experience on television.

Official AIDS figures in France start with 11 cases in 1981 (17 total cases were identified retrospectively), 959 in 1985 (including 614 among homo/bisexuals), 2,213 in 1986 (1,363 among homo/bisexuals), 4,458 in 1987 (2,614 among homo/bisexuals) and 7,503 in 1988 (4,191 among homo/bisexuals); by 1993, there were 30,616 cases of AIDS in France (14,718 among homo/bisexuals).[40] The early figures do not take account of seroconversion, nor of people with immuno-suppression. Only in 1984–85 was it confirmed that LAV (later known as HIV) was the virus responsible. Condoms only started to be seen as a means of prevention in 1984, with the AIDS test becoming available in 1985 as we have seen. By 1987, it was estimated that between 100,000 and 300,000 people were HIV-positive; out of these only 40,000 to 50,000 had been tested. By 1988, 59 per cent of cases could be found among homosexuals and bisexuals, 13.6 per cent among drug addicts and 10.2 per cent among the heterosexual population.[41]

While it is, of course, embedded in the general history of AIDS in the West, the particular history of the epidemic in France was both specific and notably disastrous. Hence the specificity of the AIDS crisis in France needs to be addressed in some detail. For example, for roughly comparable populations, the rate of incidence in France was *three times* that of the United Kingdom; there were more cases of AIDS in the Paris region than in the whole of the United Kingdom. On 30 June 1995, France had 37,000 cases (17,200 of them among homosexuals/bisexuals and 17,369 reported in Ile-de-France) and the United Kingdom 11,051 cases (7,923 of them among homosexuals/bisexuals).[42] The government faltered, and there were no community organisations and/or institutions, indeed no real sense of community among gay men, to take up the challenge, as they did in English-speaking countries when governments and public health officials defaulted.

This is due to a variety of reasons. France is a republic, based on the principles of 'Liberté, Égalité, Fraternité' ('Liberty, Equality, Fraternity'). French citizenship is seen as a 'contract resulting from a political will, from the convergence of free, individual decisions to live together according to a core of basic universal principles'.[43] This core was established to the exclusion of other principles. Indeed, going back to Ernest Renan in the nineteenth century, Caron shows how race, language and religious affinity are not seen as valid principles on which to build a nation.[44] Recent debates have shown that gender and sexual politics are at the heart of national identity, but in France sexuality is constructed as a matter of private rather than public identity.

By implication a gay 'community' would blur the boundaries between the public and the private sphere, 'a boundary on which individual freedom rests'.[45] 'Républicanisme' tends to be seen as a particularly French innovation as against 'communitarisme', an American invention[46] which, some would say, is invading France, together with political correctness. In the USA, communities have long been a part of left-wing discourses. In France, as Caron suggests, they have been associated with the extreme right from the time when Maurice Barrès 'made cultural relativism a central tenet of his nationalist politics', and regarded the notion of universal values as a dangerous invention.[47] Recent scandals in France centred on religion and immigration, such as the status of North Africans or the veil controversy (Muslim girls not being allowed to attend a French secular state school until they remove their veil), unearthed the same dichotomy: there is no room for difference within the model of republican integration. The irony is that this model does not produce integration but exclusion on the grounds of difference/otherness. In this context, the socialist government treated a *public* health emergency, the AIDS crisis, as a *private* matter for individuals.

Hargreaves points to the fact that processes of nationalism in France presuppose 'integration', as encouraged by successive socialist governments.[48] Integration presupposes assimilation and this means in turn that homosexuality can only be accepted if it remains within the boundaries of the private sphere. At the beginning of the epidemic, the virus was said mostly to be affecting gay men and drug users. Pratt shows how this triggered off identity-based concepts unfamiliar to French culture: 'In this way, the existence of the virus alone threatened to expose key assumptions about the nation as integrated group, revealing the "imagined" of the community'.[49] National integrity was seen as paramount in the fight against AIDS, at the expense of naming various groups (such as gay men and intravenous drug users) that were being infected and with whom some prevention work could have been undertaken much earlier. In the process, homosexuality was seen as incapable of being assimilated and French national identity was reaffirmed in terms of heteronormativity. Hence the AIDS

12

epidemic in France is linked to the differing conceptions of the place of communities in the Republic.

Right-wing discourses capitalised on the virus to further their agenda of national purification, homophobia and nationalism. This was not helped by the French mainstream press which referred to AIDS as the 'cancer gay' ('the gay plague') and 'La Peste de l'an 2000' ('The Plague of the year 2000').[50] A headline in *Le Matin de Paris* on 2 January 1982 read 'Les homosexuels punis ... par le cancer' ('Homosexuals punished ... by cancer'). AIDS was identified so closely with the homosexual community (hypothetical as the concept of a community was) that it was left to homosexuals to do something about it. It was only when it became clear that the heterosexual population was being infected that the government changed its policies, declaring in 1987 that AIDS had become a 'major national issue'. The Minister of Health, Michèle Barzach, claimed that HIV was now affecting the heterosexual population and talked about a race against time.[51] These facts speak for themselves: institutionalised homophobia seems to be at the root of the government's apathy. The republican model is also partly to blame for this late response: when AIDS was perceived as the issue of marginalised groups (homosexuals and intravenous drug users), the government remained apathetic; when it started to affect the *nation* (the heterosexual population), it became a 'major national issue'.

There was also a tendency to say that homosexuals got what they deserved following years of sexual liberation, and this is echoed in some of the texts under study in this volume. There was talk of innocent victims such as haemophiliacs and people who had had blood transfusions, and guilty ones such as homosexuals, intravenous drug users and prostitutes. Stereotypically, gay sex was linked with promiscuity and this presented a direct threat to the nuclear monogamous family in a country embedded in Catholicism. Indeed, the spread of the virus was facilitated by the government's reluctance to start advertising and prevention campaigns, since this would mean acknowledging the realities of gay sex. Moreover, the first prevention campaigns in 1987 were marked by an assumption of universal heterosexuality which did little to target the gay population.[52] Pratt says that homosexuals ended up being framed in France 'as the cause of AIDS, rather than the group most in need of clear information, but were also blamed for not doing enough to prevent the spread of the epidemic'.[53]

Another factor I have touched upon is the fact that France is a Catholic country. A law existed which stated that condoms could not be advertised freely, which was only lifted in 1988. The taboo surrounding gay sex was also a contributing factor in prevention campaigns. Talking about gay sex meant talking about sex which does not serve the purpose of the reproduction of the French family unit. Talking about intravenous drug users meant tackling a problem best left unspoken. The dimension of Catholic guilt came to the fore too: if one was HIV-positive, it was because somehow one deserved it. The pursuit of pleasure is closely associated with punishment (after all Adam and Eve were banished from paradise for tasting the forbidden fruit), and many of the texts under study here reflect this way of thinking: homosexuals were now getting their 'just punishment'. All the aforementioned elements contributed to a politicisation of the disease. It became a site of social and political control, 'serving to patrol, enforce or shore up senses of national identity'.[54]

In October 1990, a conference in Montreux looked at AIDS prevention. What came out of the conference was that prevention worked best in countries such as the Netherlands or the United Kingdom where gay groups have been established for many years (by comparison, Arnal refers to 1981 as the year when homosexuality in France entered the political scene and the mainstream media).[55] Other reasons advanced for the number of people infected in France were the poor hygiene of the French, a suspicion that prevention equalled repression, and the lack of any body dealing with sexual health apart from 'Planning familial' ('Family planning'), which focused exclusively on contraception issues, usually for heterosexual couples. In the early 1990s, a campaign promoting the use of condoms was stopped by Pierre Bérégovoy (in post in the socialist government at the time) because it was associated with contraception. This touched on the problem of declining birth rates in France, a very sensitive issue which managed to rally the right, Catholics and the left-wing government. This example shows clearly that ideas such as the nuclear family unite political parties across the spectrum, and it also shows how far hetero-normativity is embedded in French society under the guise of national 'identity' and equality!

Given this specific context, how did the (hypothetical) gay community react in the early years of the epidemic? The character of Foucault/Muzil says in the novel by Hervé Guibert: 'Un cancer qui toucherait exclusivement les homosexuels, non, ce serait trop beau pour être vrai, c'est à mourir de rire' ('A cancer that would affect only homosexuals, no, it would be too good to be true, I am killing myself with laughter').[56] The character Muzil has understood that society at large would like to get rid of homosexuals by inventing a disease which would strike exclusively at the heart of their population. But this reaction also captures the response of disbelief of many homosexuals at the thought of prevention: they were not required to carry a pink triangle, but they were doomed with an illness called SIDA following the previous years of sexual liberation, told to wear protection at all times, and that the best way of staying seronegative was to be in a monogamous relationship; indeed, back-rooms and saunas would eventually be closed.

There was no tradition in France of liberationist thinking and action, nor an organisable community base that would have permitted gay men, at least, to respond effectively. While in Northern Europe, Britain and the USA, there were debates about sex and gender, this was not really the case in France. After May 1968 and the militancy of the 1970s from people such as Guy Hocquenghem and the FHAR (Front Homosexuel d'Action Révolutionnaire, created in 1971 and disbanded in 1974), there was a general lack of political will. In any case the FHAR rejected 'any concept of homosexual identity and visibility', declaring that the individual is not the proper subject of politics.[57] The main movements were the CUARH (Comité d'Urgence Anti-Répression Homosexuelle, Emergency committee against homosexual repression), created in 1979 but effective from 1980, which

focused on discrimination, integration and public recognition of homosexuality, and the GLH (Groupe de Libération Homosexuelle, Group
for homosexual liberation). Following the Veil law legalising abortion
(passed in 1980), there was a tendency for feminists to disengage from
the political arena. Activism was taken up by lesbian groups in the
early 1980s but splits between separatists and non-separatists ended
up weakening the women's movement to a large extent.

Paradoxically, the fact that France had a socialist government may
have lulled the gay population into a false sense of security. The socialist
government under François Mitterrand had decriminalised homosexuality with the equal age of consent for homosexuals and heterosexuals
(15 years) introduced in 1982. Frogier believes that activism was not
easily assimilated to the socialist and productivist ideologies of the
left.[58] Interestingly, Woods reminds us that the discriminatory law
fixing the age of consent for male homosexuals at 21 was introduced in
1942 by the Vichy government to consolidate its authoritarian
credentials in the eyes of the Nazis. Unlike other laws (such as anti-
semitic laws), the article was not abolished after the Second World
War but remained until 1982. There is a direct connection here
between fascism and homophobia in French society.[59] As Savigny
analysed, one starts with AIDS, then carries on through racial,
religious, social or cultural identifiers, to exclude individuals from the
nation under the guise that it is for their own protection.[60]

This liberalising moment in French society may well have been a
double-edged sword, demobilising AIDS activists who ended up
responding very slowly to the AIDS crisis. This is now established in
books on the subject: '[…] the euphoria surrounding Mitterrand's
victory was followed by a large-scale demobilisation within all the
social movements'.[61] In 1982, what became known in France as the
Coral scandal brought issues such as paedophilia into the public domain
and served to split homosexual voices either in favour or against it.
This bitterness lingered on well into 1983 according to Martel, who
states that between 1982 and 1985, militancy was disappearing as
writers became the mouthpieces for homosexuality.[62] This was by no
means universal. Michel Foucault, for instance, decided not to present

himself as a gay militant, wary as he was of any homosexual 'identity', or of being defined by one's sexuality by society – as justified in his writings. There was no homosexual culture made visible in France in the early 1980s, unlike in the United States where, for instance, gay studies courses started to feature in universities (though Guy Hocquenghem was still a central figure for homosexual liberation in France).[63] Such a culture could have served as a useful springboard in terms of prevention in the mid-1980s as it did in other countries, and might have encouraged writers to write openly about the virus. It is no coincidence that Alain Emmanuel Dreuilhe, one of the first writers to publish a book about living with AIDS, had lived in America for a number of years, and was living in America at the time of the publication of his book. He was much more embedded in American 'communitarism' than in French 'republicanism' which perhaps makes the difference between feeling able to write the book or not. Collective struggles became a thing of the past in France in the mid-1980s and the 'commercial ghetto', symbolised by the Marais area in Paris, was now exploiting the space left vacant; the early 1980s saw the rise of individualism.[64] This was the period of Minitel cruising, chatlines and back-rooms: 'Sex acts took precedence over militant discourse; in the early 1980s, for lack of a gay political economy, a sexual community appeared in France'.[65] This is perhaps slightly exaggerated by Martel, based exclusively on Paris, and somewhat moralistic, but it may well capture the *mood* of the time.

In 1982, two doctors, Willy Rozenbaum and Jacques Leibowitch, started approaching Parisian homosexual networks to talk about the crisis in France; however, they were seen as part of the repressive discourse. A classic response was captured by a gay doctor telling Rozenbaum that disseminating information about the disease 'can be exploited by the forces of repression'.[66] While this reaction is understandable given the context highlighted above, it is also a fact that gay men desperately needed the information in order to make informed choices. Rozenbaum and Leibowitch's repeated attempts were not really effective until October 1984. By comparison, the homosexual community in the United Kingdom started reacting as early as 1982. To return to the previous line of argument regarding the wider political context of gay activism, in the United Kingdom Margaret Thatcher and the Conservatives were in power and repression was the order of the day (for example, the Parisian culture of back-rooms did not exist because of the political climate). Hence, there was no chance of militants easing off. Watney writes that harassment and homophobia resulted in 'a marked strengthening of gay community-based identities and a sense of solidarity in resistance'.[67] This phenomenon could partly explain the discrepancy in the number of people infected by HIV in these two European countries. In the United Kingdom, there were national networks such as lesbian and gay switchboards, which organised the first UK conference on AIDS in 1983 (the London switchboard was created in 1973), and the Gay Medical Association. In 1983, the Terrence Higgins Trust was founded. This AIDS organisation included non-homosexuals and became very active by means of telephone chatlines, leaflets and lobbying the government; it was also instrumental in regulating blood donation. Martel concludes that the creation of gay organisations to meet the challenge of AIDS was linked to the community structure in different countries: the Republican model (which effectively denies the existence of communities) did not react to the crisis.[68] Gay organisations began to mobilise in the Netherlands and Luxembourg (as in the United Kingdom) in 1982; in Germany and Spain in 1983; in Denmark and Italy in 1984; in Belgium and France in 1985; and in Ireland (another Catholic country) in 1986.[69]

In analysing the *Gai Pied* articles in 1982, Woods shows how complacent the main gay magazine was towards the AIDS crisis. His analysis of *Gai Pied* cartoons also highlights this complacency, and he draws a useful parallel with cartoons in the gay press in Britain and the United States which 'tended to focus less ambiguously on the failings of officialdom and the illogicality of public fears'.[70] He concludes that the early coverage of the epidemic in *Gai Pied* was characterised by suspicion of the outsider, of the institutions of heterosexuality, of the American state and of the medical establishment, while overlooking the needs of gay men themselves: 'Anti-gay paranoia had fostered paranoid gay responses'.[71] Martel gives a similar portrait of *Gai Pied* but also of the entire gay press (*Homophonies*, *Masques*, *Magazine*) for the first half of the 1980s, while making the point that their combined readership must have been around 100,000 people, a figure which could have made a difference in mobilisation against AIDS.[72] As Pratt puts it, the gay community (for there was indeed a community as the epidemiology of AIDS shows) was trapped in a double-bind in these early days where 'mention of gays as a group in the context of the epidemic would lead to discrimination against them, whereas it is actually their systematic erasure from public discourse which puts them most at risk'.[73] Gay French citizens dealt as best they could with their individual catastrophe (which included the phobic reactions of others to their disease) without, it seems, imagining forms of solidarity that might have encouraged a collective response. This is a striking feature of all the texts under study here: the narrators project a strong sense of isolation and/or solitude.

In France, the first prevention association can be credited to Daniel Defert and his friends who as early as 1984 wanted to create AIDES (a combination of AIDS and 'aide', meaning 'help' in French).[74] According-ing to Martel's account, like Rozenbaum and Leibowitch, Defert first encountered some resistance from two key players who needed to be on board if the association was to reach out to its intended audience effectively: the editors of *Gai Pied* and *Masques*.[75] AIDES came to life in November 1984 and set up telephone hotlines, distributed leaflets, organised debates and offered practical help to people affected. Rozen-baum and Leibowitch, together with Jean-Baptiste Brunet, worked closely with AIDES. The following year AIDES slowly extended its operations to other major cities in France. With hindsight, one of the main dilemmas for AIDES was that it was against the 'homosexualisation' of the association, no doubt because of homophobia, but in the end it was perceived as a homosexual organisation by the powers that decided on subsidies, and this worked to its detriment. At the same time, the gay community did not identify with AIDES at the outset for the very reason that it presented itself as including non-homosexuals. However, in 1985, *Gai Pied* started to give AIDES its support by inserting its leaflets into one of its issues; AIDES became fully operational from

1987 onwards. ACT-UP Paris was created in 1989 by Didier Lestrade, two years after ACT-UP in the United States, twenty years after the FHAR and almost ten years after the first ever mention of the disease. Frogier believes that this period sees the start of a 'homosexual community' in France, with specific campaigns demolishing the view that there was universal equality of care for PWAs in France,[76] but by then the infection rates had rocketed.

How did the socialist government react to the crisis? In 1985, when members of AIDES approached the government for a subsidy to hand out free condoms in saunas, the response from the doctor who had been put in charge of the efforts against AIDS after consulting with the government was: 'They [the prime minister's department] are stupid. But the department of the prime minister thinks that if we were to fund AIDES, we would create the impression that we were helping queers' (in French 'les pédés').[77] The same year, the government refused to change the law to allow condom advertising and the legal sale of syringes. The socialists were in a very sensitive political situation at the time. In the early 1980s, the French Communist Party and the main left-wing unions, CGT (Confédération générale des travailleurs, General confederation of labour) and Lutte Ouvrière (Workers' struggle), were still partly opposed to the demands of homosexuals, and therefore in line with the position of right-wing parties. They saw homosexuality as a capitalist defect and a petty bourgeois affectation. Legislative elections were coming up in 1986, and early indications were that it was going to be a close call. In fact, on 20 March 1986, the French national assembly's majority swung to the right and Jacques Chirac was elected prime minister. Hence a period of 'cohabitation' ensued, with President Mitterrand from the left and the prime minister and the government from the right. It could well be that leading up to the legislative elections, the government did not want to turn away potential allies by appearing to side with the unacceptable face of homosexuality, 'les pédés'. At the time the socialist government was close to the GPL (Gais pour la liberté, Gays for freedom) who earned the nickname 'la gauche caviar' (literally 'the caviar left' – similar to 'champagne socialists' in the United Kingdom) and did not want to alienate them for fear of losing their votes. Martel encapsulates their decision in the following slogan: 'the homosexual vote rather than information for gays'.[78] The socialists also believed that they would have alienated some people whose support they needed, at least for the second round of voting – members of the French Communist Party and the main left-wing unions as well as middle-of-the-road voters who were still undecided. In the end, the French government did give *some* funding to AIDES: 300,000 francs in 1985, and, in 1986, 300,000 francs with another 190,000 at the end of the year (it had been asked for 2 million francs). Mitterrand, despite being the president of France from 1981 to 1995, never made any assessment of the AIDS crisis. His first public mention of the word dates to 1993 during a televised greeting for the new year.[79] It was only in 1987 that the first government campaign took place. If we compare France with other European nations, the Netherlands had its first campaign in 1983, Denmark in 1984, Germany, Belgium, Spain and Greece in 1985, Ireland, Portugal and the UK in 1986. The French government refused until February 1986 to fund the AIDS test. The first two free testing centres were opened only in May 1987 and it was finally decided in late 1987 to open these throughout France.

In the latter part of the 1980s, there was an increase in homophobic discourses from extreme right political parties and from the Church. After the installation of the right in government in March 1986, the extreme right in France as well as some right-wing magazines such as *Le Figaro*[80] seized the opportunity to make AIDS a political issue. The most notorious statements came from Jean-Marie Le Pen (leader of the national front) and Jacques Médecin. This stance was also taken up by Charles Pasqua, Minister of the Interior, who even threatened to ban *Gai Pied*. The Church joined in too with the Pope condemning the use of condoms. Martel believes that the intransigent messages coming from the Church affected French society by mobilising Church sympathisers, and that their combined efforts were probably responsible for maintaining the ban on condom advertising until 1987.[81] Paradoxically, he believes that the political statements, especially from the national front, forced the government to dissociate themselves from these groups and to agree to advertise condoms, distribute syringes and create free testing centres.[82]

To sum up, the severity of the AIDS crisis in France was largely due to a narrow exclusive definition of nation, sidelining issues of sexual identity and making some groups invisible. The Republican model was also at the root of the decision in 1985 to refuse the legalisation of condom advertising. This was a turning point. In that year alone, official cases of AIDS in France increased by 1,254. By 1987, it was estimated that between 100,000 and 300,000 people were HIV-positive. But it had been decided that the sexual transmission of a disease was a private matter rather than a public responsibility. Allied to this was the attitude of the French government in the early 1980s which was tainted with political opportunism. Jean-Baptiste Brunet, one of the two main interlocutors between AIDES and the socialist government, said in 1991 that the government in the early 1980s gave priority to political and financial interests over a public health crisis.[83] Public health came to signify the well-being of the dominant population, that of heterosexuals. This public health crisis has been called the second national AIDS scandal in France, even greater than the contaminated blood scandal which, as I write in 2001, has not seen the main culprits brought to justice: a third trial is planned for the end of 2001, or 2002, over fifteen years after the events. But there will never even be a trial over the second national AIDS scandal in France: the rate of infection in the 1980s, especially among the homosexual population.

Before closing my introduction, I want to mention the theoretical minefield of 'AIDS and Representation', which, as Edelman notes,[84] is at the centre of debates on AIDS and postmodernism. Edelman quotes Jameson talking about the point of intersection between the two as being 'the death of the subject'.[85] Edelman sees an opportunity for AIDS to be seen as 'a crisis in [...] the social shaping or articulation of subjectivities' since it has been positioned as engaging identity as an issue.[86] He argues that anyone approaching the subject of AIDS is brought up against his or her own constitution as subject to and within ideology, further claiming that the politics of AIDS is linked to the politics of the subject.[87] There is an added difficulty linked to the specific nature of the matter under study: 'AIDS [...] resists our attempt to inscribe it as a manageable subject of writing – exceeding and eluding the medical, sociological, political, or literary discourses that variously attempt to confront or engage it'.[88] One article fleshing out the issue warns about the destruction of the text by AIDS, and its overwhelming presence both as subject and object of all discourse.[89] Another states that trying to place 'AIDS fiction within the framework of the traditional novel belies the reality of AIDS. AIDS is a tragedy pure and simple.'[90] Thus the subject-matter I am dealing with presents a challenge to the theories and methodologies of literary criticism. Do we, as some critics have done, talk about 'contaminated' texts, literature of plagues, catastrophes, pandemics; or, in Joseph Dewey's words, about a 'countermovement of eros',[91] or 'a theory of marginality, subversion, dissidence, and othering' as Diana Fuss advocates under the umbrella of lesbian and gay theory?[92] For even when particular genres are used such as the confessional/autobiographical, these are subjected 'to a series of experiments, "irreverent" challenges and constant transformations, never allowing [them] to lapse into a static formula that would lend [themselves] to generalizing categorization'.[93] According to Dollimore, 'literary theory and criticism have been unable to appreciate and do justice to these transgressions'.[94] As if this was not enough of a difficulty, I also have to take into account the more general point that 'the practice of criticism involves taking up a position on the meaning of a text and fixing it through the production of a reading'.[95] In mitigation, I would argue that because of the three techniques I use (textual commentary, psychoanalytic theory and general social/cultural comment), my reading is not fixed but multiple, reflecting both the text and my own gendered subjectivity.

We saw above that, according to Edelman, anyone approaching the subject of AIDS is brought up against his or her own constitution as subject to and within ideology. Hence, I now need to locate myself in the sites of power/knowledge/desire. In addition, I do not want to be, as Edelman puts it, a writer operating within the 'neutralizing conventions of literary criticism'.[96] I want to confront the fact that the narrative voices in the various texts under consideration are presented as those of a heterosexual woman, a bisexual woman, a heterosexual man, and three gay men, and that, in a way, *I* am speaking about all of these. I want to make clear that it is my intention to speak *about* the various authors under study, but not *for* them. I have no authority nor any special dispensation to speak on their behalf. On another level, I agree with Chambers that, as a reader of these texts, I have 'responsibilities of readerly survivorhood, which are those of ensuring the survival of the text whose author is dead, and of prolonging its witness'.[97] Reflecting further, Chambers calls this type of writing the 'witnessing of AIDS' in which critics can participate by means of their commentary, itself a process of continuity from the original text.[98] If we take the example of Simonin, the dominant discourse was so intent on making him invisible and on silencing him that, in a sense, not to speak about him would be to collude with this dominant discourse.

There is also the delicate question of why *I* should be writing specifically about AIDS.[99] On one level, almost subconsciously, all these writings affect me at a very deep level, at a point of juncture that meets with my own very early experiences of loss, and fantasised feelings about the death of the self where in order to survive psychically, I had to 'split' (which perhaps gives me some intuition for sensing when this is happening in the texts). These writings connect with an already existent pool of similar feelings, and therefore resonate deeper rather than simply touching the surface. This connection has only become apparent recently, but the underlying pull towards these writings was there from the outset, even if I was not fully conscious of it. This has allowed me, on a fantasy level, to position myself as a reader, to join in with the pain and loss, with the confrontation of Thanatos, though admittedly in a realm where I was still in control; it has provided some sort of necessary outlet. On another level, I believe in the interaction between the personal and the political; AIDS writing is a form of commitment, and I have shown elsewhere that it is for me the eighties and nineties equivalent of Sartre's notion of committed literature.[100]

Finally, it would be naïve of me not to speak of my own history of desire and not to put on record my own heterosexual boundaries as well as the way my internalised homophobia has been pushed and challenged by some of my reading. Hugo Marsan writes in the introduction to his book: 'Parler du sida, c'est dire l'homosexualité, la toxicomanie, les initiations sexuelles diverses et dévoiler ainsi les liens de fascination que l'hétérosexualité conventionnelle entretient avec les zones marginales du plaisir' ('To speak about AIDS is to talk about homosexuality, drug addiction, various sexual initiations, and thus to unveil the bonds of fascination which conventional heterosexuality invests within marginal zones of pleasure').[101]

Following on from the question of AIDS and representation, I stated that the texts under study had different categories: 'real life/true story', diary, testimony, interview, confession, autobiography. Caron makes the judicious point that the community approach to the epidemic in the United States and the view of AIDS as a personal tragedy in France reflect the different AIDS writing coming from the two countries: plays such as Larry Kramer's *The Normal Heart* are collective rituals whereas 'the (auto)biographical narrative appears to be the most appropriate literary form to convey the experience' in France.[102] In these types of narratives, we have started to problematise the issue of 'truth' following feminist poststructuralists. One is reminded of Foucault's *Power/Knowledge* in which he says that all he has ever written is fiction, before continuing: 'I do not mean to say, however, that the truth is therefore absent. It seems to me that the possibility exists for fiction to function in truth, and for bringing it about that a true discourse engenders or "manufactures" something that does not yet exist, that is, fictions it.'[103] So even when I use the word 'true' throughout this book as in 'true/real life story' or 'true incident', I am fully aware that I am dealing with *fiction* functioning in truth mode. And when one interprets stories, which is basically what I am doing throughout this book, as Freeman puts it, '[…] there is not all that much separating the interpretation of supposedly "true" stories from fictional ones'.[104] Truth and fiction are not dichotomous in my eyes; positions and meanings are both engaged in fictionalising. Walkerdine substitutes for the category of the 'real', both 'veridicality' and 'cultural forms and practices' since they both produce 'regimes of meaning, truth, representation in which there are particular relations of signification';[105] this is what I will take 'real' to mean when I use the term in this book. Finally, I concede that my own narrative around these texts could be described as fictionalising, indeed should be described as fictionalising. My own identifications may well be rooted in fantasy, but I would argue that these practices are never real outside of fantasy anyway, always governed by power and desire.

A rapid overview of the binary truth/fiction or autobiography/novel, which I see rather as fluid, does not seem to help in terms of categorising the texts under consideration or in approaching them; it rather confuses the matter. I have instead written this book in two different parts by drawing a distinction between *AIDS fiction* (Part I) and *AIDS testimony* (Part II).[106] In the corpus under study, there are some works which, despite being labelled as testimony, confession and 'real life/true story', are works of fiction: Laygues, *Sida, Témoignage sur la vie et la mort de Martin*; Juliette, *Pourquoi moi?, Confession d'une jeune femme d'aujourd'hui*; and Winer, *Bienvenue dans le monde du sida!* (although none of them bears the word 'novel' on the front cover, unlike the *novels* mentioned in note 1). These works may give the impression of relating autobiographical events, but they are highly *fictionalised*.

There are also some clearly testimonial texts, written under their authors' actual names and best described as personal testimony: Simonin, *Danger de vie*, Aron, 'Mon sida', and Dreuilhe, *Corps à Corps, Journal de Sida*. An obvious way of underlining these two separate categories is to say, with Danthe, that Laygues, Juliette and Winer all write under pseudonyms,[107] while Simonin, Aron and Dreuilhe can be identified as flesh and blood human beings who all appeared on television to talk about their serological status. Another paradoxical difference is that, to some degree, all the texts grouped as *fiction* appear to make a claim to some kind of *'truth'*: testimony, confession and 'real life/true story'. It is also interesting that the narrative voices are (at least ostensibly) those of a heterosexual woman, a bisexual woman, and a heterosexual man for the AIDS fictions, and of three gay men for the AIDS testimonies. Making this distinction between AIDS fictions and AIDS testimonies means that the latter are in line with AIDS writing in other countries and subsequent writing in France, that is, predominantly gay (an anomaly in view of the presumed gender of the authors of the AIDS fictions which I highlighted at the beginning of the introduction). The fictions are conventional in their representation (even if the story told is ostensibly 'true') and tend to reproduce the dominant discourse and most of its prejudices against PWAs; the testimonies are tentatively trying to break out of the dominant discourse, with varying degrees of success, in order to present something (in this case living with AIDS) whose reality society is trying to ignore. This latter category represents a struggle with conventional discursive means which is a sign of a desire to be 'genuine' on the part of the narrator; this desire will inevitably be flawed, but to the extent that it is readable in the narrator's difficulties, it serves as a sign of the narrative's desire for authenticity and of the narrator's wish to be a witness; 'I wanted to be a witness. It seemed to me to be an internal demand', says Aron in the epigraph to this book.

Inevitably, there is more fluidity between fiction/testimony than I have argued but the distinction provides a useful way of doing justice to the testimonial texts while not overvaluing the fictional ones. One is reminded of Edelman: '(I)n the case of AIDS, infection endlessly breeds sentences – sentences whose implication in a poisonous history of homophobic constructions assures us that no matter what explicit ideology they serve, they will carry within them the virulent germ of the dominant cultural discourse.'[108]

Part I

AIDS Fiction

1 Laygues: The Ambiguity in Witnessing

At first glance, Hélène Laygues' book, *Sida, Témoignage sur la vie et la mort de Martin*[1] seems to belong to the category of writings classified under the title 'AIDS and the Culture of Accompaniment in France', in Ross Chambers's influential article on the subject.[2] Published in 1985, the back cover tells us that the book is original since it is the first time that an account of witnessing ('témoignage') is offered by a woman whose husband has contracted the illness. Witnessing implies engagement with a subject rather than detachment, closeness rather than distance. An analysis of the book will establish whether my reading agrees with these suppositions.

Hélène Laygues, the book's author, identifies herself as the first-person narrator. On page 228, she refers to herself as 'Hélène V.' as she is introducing herself to another character, which seems to indicate that her surname does not tally with the front cover. In fact Michel Danthe claims that, according to information he obtained from a series editor working for Hachette, a pseudonym was used.[3] This confirms the trend in early AIDS writing in France where authors used pseudonyms because there were a lot of risks involved in using one's own name when talking about a subject which was generating moral panic throughout the world. Though I am aware of the theoretical distinction between the terms 'author' and 'narrator', I shall refer to Hélène as both the narrative and authorial voice, and take Hélène to represent a female voice (although this particular gender subject-position could be a gender performance),[4] knowing that the subjectivity of 'Hélène' is multi-positional, and positioned by particular discourses and practices, not least of which is my own subject-position.

How is the narrative organised? Hélène is the first-person narrator throughout the book. In Chapter 1, we learn that Martin has been dead for a year, as Hélène is relaxing with Paul, her best friend. A phone call in English interrupts their evening; 'Julian H.' an American whom Martin had met in New York wants a bed for the night, unaware that Martin is dead. They invite him in for a drink, and Hélène, referring to herself as Martin's wife, gets Paul to tell Julian in English that he has died from AIDS, inviting him in turn to be tested.

A number of things can be gleaned from this first encounter that perpetuate misconceptions surrounding HIV in France in the early 1980s. First, Hélène appears to be quite bourgeoise, not a misconception in itself but an important element of her own positioning, especially with reference to sexuality, as will become relevant later on in my analysis. Paul and even Martin, her husband, say 'vous' to her according to the dialogue reported in that first chapter. Secondly, by associating Martin with the United States, the book echoes the *Gai Pied* headline of 1982: 'US Gai Cancer',[5] confining the 'gay cancer' to America, an important factor in delaying prevention work undertaken in France.[6] Thirdly, it is made clear that Martin used to have sex with gay men, so at this stage one can only assume that he was bisexual.

As we read the following chapters, which are a series of flashbacks, the story is fleshed out. Hélène was divorced when she was 35 with an 8-year-old daughter. She is now in her early fifties and Martin was 47 when they met. She is an antique dealer. In Chapter 6, it becomes apparent that she and Martin share the same shop front, they are business associates. He furnishes Parisian apartments, often using the furniture she sells in the shop. The book then basically retraces Martin's illnesses from the very first flu-like symptoms in 1980 (p. 55), and the first headaches in 1982 (p. 56) when the narrator is effectively speculating about when Martin was infected (during a trip to the United States she assumes),[7] to the bitter end (p. 288).

The central imagery patterns of 'front/back' take us into a deeper understanding of the book. For there is, throughout, a contrast between what appears to be going on, and what is in fact going on, the shop front or façade and the interior. My contention is that *Sida, Témoignage sur la vie et la mort de Martin* is anything but a witnessing, an accompanying of Martin in his life and death. Rather, it revolves around Hélène, and her ambivalent foray, as a bourgeoise heterosexual woman, into the world of what she sees as transgressive sexuality, namely gay sex. There is also an element of voyeurism in the book, which will be explored in my argument. A collision of different discourses is apparent, based on a conflict between different subject-positions, as well as, at times, some degree of collusion; the heterosexual bourgeois Parisian world telescoping with a certain type of gay lifestyle linked to adventurous desire. These two worlds are usually sealed off from each other; their encounter produces the underlying tension, a friction – and at times a *frisson* – between *dominant* (representing) and *subordinated* (represented) discourses; hence we are dealing here with shifting subject-positions. Connell reminds us that the very existence of homosexual masculinity is a destabilising 'subversion' in patriarchal society.[8]

A second encounter also takes place in the book. In 1982, the French gay newspapers *Arcadie* and *Gai Pied* clashed. The clash was one of culture between two different types of homosexual politics, as described by Gregory Woods's article.[9] The 'Arcadia type' was quick to condemn types of sexuality different from theirs, encapsulated by what Woods calls 'history lessons' on Greek love;[10] *Gai Pied* represented gay liberationist politics. All of Hélène's homosexual friends belong to the Arcadia type, except for Martin. As she reminisces about meeting Paul, who will become her best friend, Hélène writes that one can be a young man who likes boys without being a pervert (p. 73). This seems to propose a hierarchy of acceptable and unacceptable homosexuality, establishing clear boundaries. Acceptability assumes assimilability, hence there are aspects of homosexuality but not of queerness which are assimilable. In her analysis of British new right discourse on sexuality, Anna Marie Smith talks about differentiating otherness as a strategy for neutralising the subversive threat of that otherness.[11] This strategy is illustrated by Paul's feelings towards men who go to a sauna to have sex: 'Ce sont des analphabètes pervers qui ne connaissent de l'amour que le rapport trou-bite!' (p. 114) ('They are illiterate perverts whose only knowledge of love is prick/hole intercourse!'). Raw sexuality is condemned, and love is defined as some kind of supreme knowledge, presumably the exclusive domain of the educated. The subversion apparent in mentioning forms of sexuality other than the 'Arcadia' type is symbolically neutralised by labelling them as perverse/perverted.

If I now return to the central organising themes of the book, it seems by the end of Chapter 6 that Martin is gay rather than bisexual, that he has a partner named Brian, and that they have an open relationship. In fact, we learn that Martin spends most of his nights in the back-rooms. The professional boundary between Hélène and Martin shifts earlier on in their association. As soon as Martin ends up sharing his love life with her, Hélène imperceptibly enters a world that both repulses and fascinates her. The marriage between Hélène and Martin appears to be a mystery (it will only be explained in Chapter 29, half-way through the book), and as readers we conclude at this stage that the book is not what it claims to be on the back cover, and that Hélène does not appear to be the witness (the spouse of an HIV-positive husband) she says she is.[12]

Throughout the narrative, there exists a tension between images of front and back, dressing up a front, presenting a fake front, and a tension between colliding and colluding. What is at work is a 'respectable' bourgeois imagination, regulated by its very strict boundaries, rooted in Catholicism and occupying a dominant discursive position partly because it oppresses minority groups perceived as subordinate, especially women, which defend their regimes of adventurous desire. In order to advance my argument, I propose to look at Hélène's treatment of Martin, and, by extension, at her relationship with adventurous desire, since I have established that this is primarily what Martin symbolises for her.

As a general rule, Hélène defends Martin when he is attacked by her other close friends such as Paul (pp. 114, 126, 136), Pierre (p. 128), and 'Madame di C.' (p. 91). The main point of their attack is that Martin has got what he deserves because of his 'rampant' sexuality. The level of their compassion is illustrated by Paul (the Arcadia-type and her best friend) who describes Martin as a 'fleur de back-room, inculte et nymphomane' (p. 52) ('back-room flower, ignorant and nymphomaniac'). But Hélène also allows herself to criticise and judge Martin, as when she is talking to Julio, one of her homosexual Arcadia-type friends. She claims that Martin has got what he deserves with what she describes in her own words as his wild sexual encounters where one risks being mugged or catching the illness (AIDS), and that at the age of 45 he should have known better (p. 96). She also criticises him to his face on more than one occasion (pp. 163, 170–71).

I have tentatively identified the main imagery of front/back in the book. This has set up a binary opposition. However, this opposition should be qualified into a more fluid mode in the postmodern tradition. For I do not believe that discourses exist simply as bipolar relations. They are according to Foucault 'tactical elements or blocks operating in the field of force relations'.[13] What is at stake is shifting boundaries and policing borders (the title of the recent book *Border Patrols*, by Steinberg, Epstein and Johnson, expresses this idea).[14] Peter Redman's chapter in this book, 'Invasion of the Monstrous Others: Heterosexual Masculinities, the "AIDS Carrier" and the Horror Genre',[15] offers a way of making sense of the apparent ambivalence in Hélène's treatment of Martin, and by extension of her version of adventurous desire. As Redman reminds us, using Stallybrass and White's *The Politics and Poetics of Transgression*,[16] the very act of repudiating in others desires which are threatening to the self is a form of ownership: 'The result of this is that the Others excluded as most threatening become simultaneously desirable'.[17] Hélène is attracted by ruthless hedonistic pleasure, defined against bourgeois morality which, though hypocritical in its gender relations, is all about maintaining an acceptable front and keeping women mostly as Madonnas. Put simply: she can allow herself to criticise Martin when she frightens herself with the results of his nocturnal wandering, but when others criticise him, it is a part of her (albeit conceivably at a subconscious level) which is rejected, and therefore she defends him and metaphorically *herself*. Some of this defence can manifest itself psychosomatically, showing that it comes from *within* Hélène. When Pierre claims that a self-proclaimed dandy such as Martin could have had the decency to commit suicide rather than rot in his bed (p. 128), she has palpitations.

The following example is a good illustration of Hélène's fragile balancing act between complicity and rejection, ultimately linked to policing her own gender position, that is, her gendered subjectivity. One day, Martin seeks her help because he wants to make a party dress for himself. This seems to be too much for Hélène. First, she has a stiff drink in order to keep her composure. Later, while the dress is being fitted, Martin strips naked in front of Hélène. She records being shocked by this, offering the explanation that he has become an imaginary woman, before commenting to herself that the size of his penis is 'very average'; later on she will keep in her mind the image of his penis as crippled ('estropié', p. 46). At the end of the fitting session, she suddenly finds herself feeling uncomfortable, looking at his face with its thick moustache and his naked shoulders, and writing: 'Cette robe ultra-féminine n'est plus une parodie cocasse mais le travestissement vénéneux d'un inverti vieillissant et pervers' (p. 46) ('This ultra-feminine dress is no longer a comical parody but the poisonous fancy dress of a perverse and ageing homosexual'). It seems as if Hélène cannot tolerate gender crossing, which is perverse in her eyes. What seems to disturb her is the fact that the symbol of the heterosexual woman's display (the dress), her own seductive 'weapon', is 'stolen' by Martin. This example illustrates Judith Butler's assertion that gender is performative, using the analogy of the drag performance.[18] In a subsequent article, Butler further clarifies: '[...] moreover, I argued that gender is produced as a ritualized repetition of conventions, and that this ritual is socially compelled in part by the force of a compulsory heterosexuality'.[19] In this case, Martin is transgressing conventions.

In another episode, Hélène recounts going for a drink in the apartment shared by Brian and his new lover Daniel. Describing Daniel serving the drinks, she writes that he was like the young woman of the house (p. 191). Yet again, this observation is a clear case of Hélène's setting boundaries and of her being disturbed by a man taking over what she sees as the hostess role. She is also reinforcing heterosexual stereotypes imposed on gay couples, with the idea that one is the symbolic male who wears the trousers, and the other is effeminate. Hélène finds her gendered identity (which generates in her, according to Butler's analysis, the illusion of an 'inner gender core',[20] or an 'essence' in hegemonic conservative discourses) threatened by Martin's dressing up and by Daniel's acting the hostess. She needs to reaffirm border delineations in view of the fact that her own gendered boundaries are being disrupted and to reassert, as Butler says, compulsory heterosexuality. She wants to fix the signified, to define meaning on behalf of particular power relations and social interests which serve the dominant discourse.

Very early in their relationship, Hélène is aware of Martin's 'promiscuity', which she sees as being closely tied into adventurous desire. At times she defends him in front of others, at other times she makes plain that it is because of his sexual behaviour that Martin has AIDS. Hence *Sida, Témoignage sur la vie et la mort de Martin* is a narrative that illustrates the idea of AIDS as punishment, the idea, with its narrative implications, that PWAs deserve to become infected because of behaviour judged extreme or otherwise unacceptable. This positions monogamous heterosexuality as the acceptable behaviour and echoes Catholicism with the idea of *just* punishment, as in original sin; according to Catholics, human beings are not on earth to enjoy themselves, but to seek redemption. Furthermore, Simon Watney has pointed out that 'The entire discourse of AIDS turns round the rhetorical figure of "promiscuity" [...] as if AIDS were related to sex in a quantitative rather than a qualitative way [...] "promiscuity" is being employed [...] as a sign of homosexuality itself, of forbidden pleasure, of *threat*.[21] Redman writes, 'The "promiscuous" person suggests a figure who refuses to respect boundaries, by insisting on uncontrollable and uncontained sexual contact', reinforcing my reading in terms of threatened boundaries.[22]

Hélène's two best friends are 'homosexual men' ('Paul' and 'Pierre B.'), bourgeois, educated, with their hearts ruled by reason rather than by their instincts, according to the female narrator (p. 37); she identifies with them. During their dinner parties, they gossip about Martin and talk about his sexual performance. Her response to this subject of conversation is worth noting: 'Ces performances me laissent rêveuse; je sonde mes souvenirs… Ai-je été aussi brillante? Humblement je dois dire que non' (pp. 36–37) ('These performances leave me dreaming; I trawl my memory… Was I equally brilliant? With modesty, I must answer no'). What is important here is that the story of Martin's 'promiscuity' gives her some form of legitimacy to daydream about sexual performance. She is getting some sexual arousal by proxy. She can only fulfil her desire vicariously.[23]

Elsewhere, she will describe her conversations with Martin as always being either about his relationship with Brian or about homosexual sexuality, commenting that the latter gave her vertigo, and describing her accompanying him along this path as both difficult and fertile (p. 168); 'difficult' and 'fertile' reflect her own ambiguity: she has to go against her own education and tradition in order to get a sense of pleasure. 'Vertigo' is a sensation of whirling, boundarylessness creates a sense of confusion. 'Fertile' suggests that the topic of conversation is finding an echo in her: she is being fulfilled in some way by talking about homosexual sexuality. In another place, she uses the expression 'wandering nights' ('nuits d'errance', p. 120) to describe Martin's night life. Unlike most of her other references to these activities, which are judgemental, one can sense here a craving for a forbidden action (what Watney calls 'forbidden pleasure') reminiscent of the nineteenth-century Baudelairian flâneur. The redefinition of boundaries has a liberating effect, so that, paradoxically, it is in the very act of erring that one may find a satisfactory set of positionings. Hélène is caught between two discourses: restrained bourgeois values, and unpoliced desires as symbolised in her eyes by her fantasy projections about Martin. At this stage, it looks as if she is flirting with the idea of sexual freedom, through voyeurism.

I now propose to pause in order to reflect on Hélène's condition (in the Marxist sense of the word). I don't want to underestimate the essentialist trajectory of desire(s) for a woman like Hélène who is effectively caught in a gender trap. A provincial puritan as she describes herself, taught not to like men, but to look upon them as procreators (p. 37), probably never allowed the opportunity to explore her own sexual orientation, stifled as she is by religion and bourgeois morality, she is trapped in a binary system, a predetermined set of discourses which correspond to her social class. This is most evident in her social make-up, which I will explore next.

There is a constant wish from Hélène to be seen as the 'good' mother to all the homosexual friends she has. She herself talks about being a mother figure to Martin (pp. 20–21), albeit at times an oppressive one (p. 105), and to Paul (p. 77), whom she has loved like the son she has never had (p. 115). She is deriving some form of power from 'caring' for men in such a way, reaffirming her own gendered subjectivity. But she is also perpetuating the stereotype of women as mothers/nurturers, leaving men as active agents outside of the home.[24] In defining herself as the 'good' mother, she is defining herself against her own mother, whom she sees as the 'bad' mother; her father apparently judged her mother to be tyrannical towards Hélène without any good reason (p. 205).

One of the blind spots in the book occurs when Hélène regrets having moulded her own daughter and Paul into heartless people without an ounce of pity or tolerance (p. 116). This echoes her own mother's values (and also her own description of herself as a young girl, as brought up by her own mother, p. 213), and it is clear from this passage that she takes responsibility for their being as they are. In pointing to how she changed as a child, however, she claims that she was taught pity (p. 213), the very quality she sees as missing in both Paul and her daughter. In order to explain this blind spot, my argument is that what is at stake is a dynamics of splitting between 'good' and 'bad' object, as in the theory of Melanie Klein.[25] The good object is Hélène and the bad object is her mother. She constantly defines herself against her mother. In one way, she must hope that the book paints her devotion to Martin in stark contrast with the attitude of her daughter (whose name we never learn) and of Paul, who paradoxically both appear to have been made in the same mould as her own mother.

We have just seen that in pinning down what changed her attitude as a child, Hélène has chosen the concept of 'pity'. I would like to analyse the choice of this concept since it will take us again into the realm of boundaries. 'Pity' is not the same as empathy or compassion. In the latter cases, one tries to put oneself in the Other's predicament, to situate oneself within the discourse position of the other. In the case of pity, one stays *within one's own clear boundaries* and reaches out towards the Other from a position of strength (it is indeed a much-praised Catholic value). In an article dealing with perceptions of HIV/AIDS, Judith Williamson denounces terror and pity as 'produced through the centuries-old generic structures that dominate our popular culture, and within it, AIDS speech' because they exclude other emotions such as, for instance, anger.[26] As Hélène puts it in a poignant moment, referring to Brian and herself: 'Martin demandait de l'amour, nous ne donnions que de l'affection' (p. 122) ('Martin wanted love, we only gave affection'). Clearly, *Sida, Témoignage sur la vie et la mort de Martin* does not portray what Chambers calls the relation of relay, which involves a sense of mutuality that implies taking unlimited responsibility.[27]

In fact, we never hear Martin's side of the story. He is not allowed his own voice. Hélène's story dominates the narrative. What we have is a heterosexual, HIV-negative viewpoint expressed in a female narrative voice, on the life and death of a gay male PWA. As readers, we are encouraged to follow Hélène's fantasy projection about Martin. The narrative perspective presents us with distancing devices designed to negate any empathy with Martin. This of course could be the reason behind the narrator/author's being presented as a heterosexual female. This book is the first ever 'witness' account to be published in France, and its marketing calculation may be that the device of using 'Hélène' will allow many readers to identify and sympathise with the narrator, and not to be alienated by Martin. We can glean from Martin's own struggle, and it is certainly ratified by the narrator, that he is a 'difficult' patient, a state of being which Chambers identifies as a form of resistance, and by implication social resistance, when analysing *Unbecoming* by Eric Michaels.[28] Whether Martin is resisting or not is something that cannot be established from the text since Martin does not have a voice. What is almost certain is that at one stage he decides to starve himself to death, but Brian and Hélène make the decision to have him admitted to a special clinic that will force-feed him. As we have seen above with respect to the Arcadia-type of homosexuality to which most of Hélène's friends belong, the text polices homosexual boundaries by splitting off good/bad gay men. It also confirms the marginalisation gay voices underwent in France in the late 1980s: it is only if they are expressed by the dominant discourse of compulsory heterosexuality that gay voices can have a say, at the risk of being distorted, fantasised or resubordinated, and in all cases neutralised; they are also framed by the 'just punishment' narrative.

As for Hélène, the question is does she succeed at all in pushing back the limits of her class and gender boundaries? Evidently, she seems to respond almost always to the men she interacts with by telling them what they want to hear, as a 'properly' brought-up woman from her class. This positioning of herself as the 'good' mother gives her power over all these homosexual men. But she then confides to the narrative what she really wants to tell them. This can range from the trivial (feeling that Martin's jumper is too bright for him but telling him that it really suits him, p. 50) to important matters (despite her feelings, she clamps down on Paul who has insulted Martin and other men like him, reserving her venom towards Paul *for the narrative*: '[…] j'eus envie de lui dire' (p. 115) ('[…] I would have liked to tell him')). It can also verge on the nasty; when Martin complains about having no male visitors in hospital, she wonders whether she should tell him the 'truth': that he has loved sexual organs rather than men, and penises don't have legs and don't visit; she in fact replies that Brian is a faithful daily visitor (p. 124). In all cases, she confides what she thinks through the narrative. It is as if she has to keep up a front of politeness, and leave her own true feelings in her head, or put them down on paper. Only as a narrator (therefore fictional by definition) and in her narrative can she exist in a mode that satisfies her.

Perhaps not surprisingly, in a chapter where there is such a criss-crossing of different discourses, I would like to offer two different conclusions. The first one will explore Hélène's collusion with adventurous desire by way of voyeurism, and the second one the collision of two different worlds.

Referring to Martin's sexual encounters, Hélène talks about fucked buttocks (though the French uses an ellipsis: 'des fesses enf...', p. 53), adding that this has nothing to do with 'la transgression suprême' ('the ultimate transgression'). Two things can be gleaned from this passage. First of all, Martin's, and by extension gay men's, pursuit of the ultimate transgression is a projection of Hélène's. Secondly and by implication, in 'accompanying' Martin, it seems obvious that it is in fact Hélène who thinks she is acting out transgressively. If we now revisit the marriage between them, the façade is a business deal. But Hélène does not miss an occasion to say *my* husband (p. 132), calling him 'darling' (p. 106), even to the American visitor after Martin has been dead for a year (p. 14). By then there is no need to protect the business arrangement at the root of the marriage.

My contention is that Hélène is in fact committing what she perceives as the ultimate transgression: a heterosexual bourgeoise marrying an HIV-positive gay man. Such a subject-position has some advantages for her: it allows her to 'accompany' Martin until his death, in some voyeuristic way, where she can also flirt with adventurous desire, albeit by proxy, while having a respectable front; and it furnishes her with the ultimate caring role of the devoted self-sacrificial, long-suffering spouse. I would concede, however, that some of what I have just articulated may be at the level of the subconscious in Hélène.

The following example will explain, I hope, how quick Hélène is in reclaiming her identity. Weedon reminds us that '[...] hegemonic conservative discourses [...] deny the possibility of changing social relations by appealing to the essential fixity of human nature'.[29]

Martin has to be hospitalised again and he wants an individual room. Hélène sees a female doctor, a complete stranger, whom she describes as having a contemptuous look on her face when she finds out that Martin is HIV-positive. Immediately, she tells the doctor that she married him out of friendship before adding: 'A part ses mœurs, il est bon et droit. Sans cela je ne serais pas ici ce soir' (pp. 236–37) ('Apart from his sexual orientation, he is good and straight. Otherwise I wouldn't be here tonight'). What she is articulating here is that, *despite* being Martin's wife, *she* belongs to the respectable world, and that *because* of his sexual orientation, *Martin* is 'bad' and 'bent' (the opposites of 'good' and 'straight'). She knows what she has to say in order to keep the sympathy of the female doctor. Such reactionary language unmasks the self-deceit entailed in her own 'transgression' in marrying him: she is sending the female doctor a powerful message while blowing her own cover. She firmly belongs to the world of respectable Catholic heterosexuals with their morality; she is one of 'them', so the doctor's contempt should not be directed towards her; she is an undercover spy in the world of the Other. What can now be crystallised is that throughout the book Hélène is being transgressive by proxy (and on paper with her marriage certificate) while still keeping up appearances, or a façade. Ultimately, her positioning on the side of moral values will take over from her adventurous side.

My second set of concluding remarks look at the collision aspect. Whenever Hélène sets clear boundaries, taking textual revenge, this is translated by a tone clearly devoid of ambiguity. We are no longer even in the realm of collision but of open confrontation. One of these areas of collision regards anal sex.[30] Once again (and cheaply), it is a question of the relationship between front and back. Hélène is doing her own internal self-policing, reinforced by her religious beliefs. This intransigence is by far the most alarming aspect of the book, which I will now explore, as it cuts right across the title of the book and the claims of its cover blurb.

When Martin gets herpes in his rectum, she gratuitously asserts that the reason why he is not talking to his doctor about it is that he feels shame. She then quotes a religious text about punishment for men who sleep with other men, and concludes: 'Le sexe interdit pourissait. La représentation symbolique du châtiment était frappante' (p. 221) ('The forbidden sexual organ was rotting. The symbolic representation of punishment was striking'); yet again, the just punishment narrative is being imposed on Martin's story. In the next paragraph, she wonders whether that is how Martin interpreted the herpes, and says that she is inclined to believe it is. Apart from her own intentionality in interpreting Martin's thought ('Je le croirais *volontiers* [...]', p. 222, my emphasis), two facts are certain: first, she is projecting onto Martin what she thinks; second, we never do find out what Martin actually feels or why he delayed telling his doctor about the herpes. The clear message in the text is that anal intercourse is outlawed as out of bounds. Elsewhere, Hélène will talk about the person that infected Martin as 'le Malin [...] le Mal' (p. 289) ('Satan [...] the Devil').[31]

A second episode situated near the end of the book is again an illustration of Hélène's imposition of her own values and boundaries on homosexual men. In a telling passage, she takes Ray, Paul's new partner, to visit Martin, literally on his deathbed. She has engineered this on purpose; she wants to protect Paul, and therefore wants Ray once and for all to understand what could happen to him if he strays (though there is absolutely no evidence in the text that he is not committed to a monogamous relationship with Paul, and hence this could be another of her fantasies about homosexual sexuality. There is no evidence either as to how and with whom Martin got infected; for all we know it could have been from a syringe, for instance, or through a blood transfusion.) At one point in the visit when Ray is at his most vulnerable (having realised that Martin is dying), she writes: 'J'avais, entre les mains, un long fouet [...] avec l[e]quel on apprend à valser aux chevaux de cirque' (p. 281) ('I had, between my hands, a long whip [...] with which one teaches circus horses to waltz'). Striking the typical attitude of a dominatrix, she is measuring her power over gay men; she wants to teach Ray a lesson. The imagery is powerful: a wild horse would represent unbridled sexuality; a circus horse trained to waltz would have had all his natural instincts whipped out of him. Hélène is perhaps angry here with what bourgeois society has made of her, but yet again, she expresses her feeling, this time anger, by turning it on others. Her 'front' motive is that she is doing what she is doing out of love for Paul. But there is no regard here for the fact that Martin's human dignity is being stripped by Ray's visit: Martin's dying moments are made a spectacle for the benefit of a complete stranger, or rather for the benefit of Hélène who wants to teach Ray a lesson.

The back cover of the book tells us that since AIDS has surfaced, the West seems to have rediscovered a taste for medieval fright, 'devious' sexuality becoming a mortal sin, a major taboo, open to the most unfortunate prejudices; it is against this state of ignorance and rumours that Laygues' book is defined. But when one actually reads the last two passages I have just quoted, it is obvious that the blurb does not tally with the narrative itself: the narrator is clearly *adding* prejudice. As Weedon reminds us, 'Within Catholicism there are subject positions which validate and even celebrate particular modes of femininity, for instance, an approach to traditional family life [...] in the case of female sexuality, for example, sex is defined as naturally heterosexual and procreative and femininity is implicitly masochistic';[32] hence the apparent self-sacrificial positioning of Hélène – though we have seen in reality how powerful she actually is, both in the story and as omnipotent narrator. Again, when reflecting on Martin's life one year after his death, Hélène writes that making inferences from what he said at different times, she is *certain* he saw his illness as a price to pay for his life of pleasure (p. 80); again the theory of the just punishment emerges. There is absolutely no shred of evidence in the text that justifies Hélène's statement; she is putting words into Martin's mouth, literally from beyond the grave. But this message echoes the last phrase of the back cover text describing sexuality as a dangerous business. Hence the message of the book is aimed at us readers, and not just at Ray; symbolically, it is us that Hélène has dragged to Martin's bedside to teach a lesson. And this is the moral lesson that the publisher endorses. Rather than a witness account, the first ever AIDS fiction published in France has turned out to be a morally and sexually repressive statement.

2 Juliette: Masculinist Desires and Sexualities

Pourquoi moi?[1] is the first account by a woman of having contracted the HIV virus to be published in France. As I mentioned in the introduction, there is a possibility that a male author is masquerading behind the female voice, but there is no evidence to indicate this. Let us assume for a moment that the story may be an invention, as Mirko Grmek believes it is.[2] This does not prevent it from carrying a level of significance since the story is presented as something that actually took place. The first-person narrator positions herself in relation to a particular set of discourses and their ensuing practices, and is also produced by these. She is also positioned by the framework of the back cover blurb. In addition, as Freeman reminds us, '[...] there is not all that much separating the interpretation of supposedly "true" stories from fictional ones'.[3] In the absence of any evidence to the contrary, I will take Juliette, the first-person narrator, as representing a female voice.

The book's full title is *Pourquoi moi? Confession d'une jeune femme d'aujourd'hui* (*Why me? Confession of a young woman of today*). Juliette is both the pseudonym of the author and the name of the narrator. She receives an anonymous phone call on Christmas day, when she is nearly 29 (it must be Christmas 1985 since Juliette was born in 1957). The caller tells her that she, like the woman who is phoning her, is likely to die since they have both shared the same lover, 'Pierre T.', though the fact that he is dying of AIDS-related illnesses is only revealed on page 89. There follows a succession of flashbacks leading to Juliette's meeting with 'Pierre T.', interspersed with moments from her childhood and the occasional catching up of the story in 1985. The narrator looks at her childhood, her teenage years and her time at university. She then gives an insider's view of the political and journalistic worlds she enters. Starting at the bottom of the ladder, she quickly moves from being a provincial freelance to writing for a Parisian magazine. At the height of her career, she moves to political journalism on radio, where she is responsible for a daily political commentary in the morning on the most important French station (France-Inter), which almost the entire nation seems to listen to, as well as a programme on television. She is cultivated by ministers, for her daily political thought for the day seems to be an important event capable of influencing French voters. This reads like the pinnacle of power and Juliette is not yet 29.

Throughout the book, there is a graphic account of her entire sexual history. Bisexual – though predominantly heterosexual – she leads a very active sex life without using any form of protection, occasionally prostituting herself, sleeping with at least one bisexual man and with promiscuous men, one-night stands; Juliette's sexual history is a real nightmare for any epidemiologist studying her case history.

The main part of *Pourquoi moi?* deals with Juliette's life before her diagnosis, up to page 127 where the second part of the book starts. I said above that her book has been written retrospectively, from her hospital bed after she has been admitted with AIDS-related illnesses. There is no indication that Juliette kept a diary; her account therefore has to rely on her memory; it is also influenced by her state of mind at the time of writing, which is the point when it is constructed. Very little is learnt about the attitude of the people surrounding Juliette since she only tells people she is HIV-positive at the end of the book.

In an 'Avertissement au lecteur' (Foreword to the reader), written by another person, we learn that she wants to remain anonymous for the time being, that she felt it necessary to give a 'brutal account' of her experience, and that she is not interested in scandal but in showing and telling. My approach in this chapter will be not to treat Juliette as a fixed individual, trapped in binary oppositions, but to try and gain some understanding of her experience from the evidence available in *Pourquoi moi?* The first foray into this will concentrate on Juliette and masculinist desires.

The book opens with an account of Juliette as a very young child climbing a steep staircase, elated by her action and defiant of her mother's voice telling her that she risks a serious injury; 'À moi, cela n'arrivera pas' (p. 11) ('It won't happen to me') is what she tells herself. In many ways, this childhood anecdote is emblematic of the entire book. Juliette, in a traditional masculinist way, reads desire as transgression and danger, and more importantly she reads transgression and desire as without consequences. There is, of course, nothing 'wrong' with women reading desire as transgression and danger, but it is usually a territory that has been colonised by men, as in the example of joyriders who tend to be almost exclusively male teenagers. We will see in Chapter 3 that there are remarkable parallels between Juliette's story and that of Mike Winer. Accomplishing the forbidden gesture of climbing the staircase gives a delighted intensity to her action. Desire is heightened by going against the familiar rules of the mother. In the same vein, Juliette's first experience of sexual intercourse is with the mayor of the local commune, also a member of parliament and a political councillor, aged over 50, and held in high esteem by local people. She is 15 years old and decides to lose her virginity to someone with experience but also with whom there is no risk of falling in love. This first encounter is described as brief and brutal. The two then meet nightly throughout the summer, and she writes matter of factly that by the end of the summer, she knows what there is to know about her body, in what she considers to be no more and no less than an apprenticeship (pp. 51–52). There is a real purpose and detachment to her attitude. This episode, of course, could fall within the legal definition of sexual abuse because Juliette is under-age, though she takes pains to recreate the incident as one in which she is in charge and knows full well what she is doing. She is pursuing power, as she lucidly points out later on in the book, albeit by proxy:

> Ce qui m'avait attirée et retenue tout un été auprès de Charles R., c'est qu'il était aussi maire, député. Je comprenais que jamais, pour moi, un homme ne serait que son corps. Qu'il faudrait que je sache, pour être émue, que ce visage soit connu, que cette main soit puissante et cette voix écoutée par d'autres hommes. (p. 55)

> What had attracted me and kept me for a whole summer with Charles R. was the fact that he was also a mayor and an MP. I understood that a man would never be only his body for me. I would have to know, in order to be moved, that his face was familiar, that his hand was powerful and that his voice was listened to by other men.

This episode – the virginal girl seeking out sexual knowledge – is very characteristic of the pornographic tradition in France. Her name too, with echoes of some of the Marquis de Sade's books, is also a clue, perhaps, that the genre here is that of soft porn, presumably addressed to male readers. In this case, Juliette's masculinist desires would be constructed in order to feed male fantasy. And this would in turn give some weight to the argument that behind the author, Juliette, there is a male writer.

But other aspects of the text seem to show that Juliette attempts to break from traditional gender roles and tries to change the power balance through sexuality. Extreme examples of such actions are when she prostitutes herself. During her first act of prostitution, where she uses no condoms, she oscillates between terror and excitement, stating that the terror is part of her excitement (p. 59), and that she is crossing boundaries (p. 64). She imagines being Jane Fonda in the film *Klute*, one of her favourite films, in which the actress plays a prostitute; Juliette says she is her own spectator watching herself in a movie. Such a description is the epitome of someone who is detached from herself, or split, in psychoanalytical terms. When her first client drops her off, she says that her fright has disappeared and that she feels no shame, writing: 'J'étais libre, forte, souveraine' (p. 62) ('I was free, strong, sovereign'). Her second act of prostitution springs a surprise on her: 'Max F.', one of her university tutors, also a local politician and a barrister, approaches her in his car as she stands on the pavement. After a night in which he reveals a taste for domination and which Juliette says brings her to new depths of fulfilment, she makes sure she helps herself to his wallet and leaves it open on the table. This gesture is doubly significant: she wants him to know what she has done, and she needs to prove to herself that she is still independent despite abandoning herself to him during the night. They continue to see each other for months, but every single time she insists that he pays her.

Coria reminds us of the sexualised nature of money and its association with manhood and virility.[4] Collecting the banknotes from her first 'trick', Juliette says that normally she could not care less about being paid, but that the money is the proof of her power (p. 62). As for 'Max F.', Juliette ends up dominating him totally, and he becomes very needy, even asking her to marry him. Lynne Segal writes in *Slow Motion: Changing Masculinities, Changing Men*, '[...] for many men it is precisely through sex that they experience their greatest uncertainties, dependence and deference in relation to women [...]'.[5] Juliette calls this sexual dependency the 'real power' women can have over men (p. 58). Payment is another way of exercising control and of removing feelings from the sexual transaction (feelings which are perhaps just underneath the surface). Juliette is turning the tables on the conventional traffic with women and subverting masculinist desires. Sexuality as a survival technique is more often associated with men than with women. In Segal's analysis, male sexual discourse tends to be domineering, denying need and vulnerability, while women deny their own power in sexual relationships.[6] Thus Juliette appears to be turning the tables on the men she encounters, refusing to endorse the myth of the link between sexuality and male dominance.[7]

In *The Bonds of Love: Psychoanalysis, feminism and the problem of domination*,[8] Jessica Benjamin denounces the fact that for Freud, sexually speaking, women's status is that of objects. But she also acknowledges, '[…] we are nevertheless obliged to confront the painful fact that even today, femininity continues to be identified with passivity […]'.[9] It is as if Juliette picks up early in life that her mother embodies passive desire. Furthermore, since the father stands for subjectivity and desire at the level of culture,[10] some women idealise men because they seem to possess what they, as women – culturally speaking – can never have: 'power and desire'.[11] It is undeniable that Juliette is strongly attracted to men in power; in fact, the more power the better. For example, having slept with Henry who is in charge of a television channel, Juliette decides that professionally he is over the hill and that she needs to move on from him. She therefore ends their sexual relationship in order to concentrate her energies on 'Michel B.', who is the managing director of the radio station, a personal friend of some cabinet ministers and even of the prime minister. Her list of conquests reads like a crescendo of power: mayor, university lecturer and local politician, cabinet minister. Never more so than when she sleeps with the cabinet minister. She knows she is being set up, but she plays along, and when they end up in bed, she appears not to hold back during their night of sex. It is as if 'the possession of the penis/phallus […] represents and relates to desires to be positioned like a man'.[12] Pierre Bourdieu shows that this attitude is anchored in socialisation whereby men are encouraged to pursue power games, and women to seek men who like power games.[13] For him, male charisma is the charm of power and the seductive dimension which having power gives.[14]

Let us come back to the notion of the sexual predator, of the 'sexy woman'. Benjamin remarks that such a woman is very often *an object*, rather than *a subject*, expressing 'not so much *her* desire as her pleasure in being desired'.[15] For Benjamin, feminist theory must not be satisfied with a simple reversal that leaves the terms of the sexual polarity intact.[16] In order to look further at the question of Juliette, masculinist desires and sexualities, I need to introduce the concept of perversion.

In *Mother, Madonna, Whore*,[17] Estela V. Welldon looks at perversion in women. In psychoanalytic terms, it means 'the dysfunction of the sexual component of personality development' (p. 6). At the root of this type of behaviour is the child's experience of infantile fear and impotence with the mother. In most cases, this is caused by an imaginary relationship with a fantasised omnipotent mother. As the mother's part-object, the child cannot exist as a separate individual, regardless of whether she is unwanted or totally identified with her mother's life (p. 9).

The inability to create subject–subject relationships can manifest itself as promiscuity (Welldon), which would fit in with Juliette's sexual life. This type of behaviour corresponds to a compulsive and illusory attempt to create object-relationships which are in fact doomed to failure (p. 48). These feelings can also be manifested in later life through cruel dominance: 'the prostitute's client or the mother's child'.[18] At this stage, it is important to stress that this behaviour is typical of children who have been sexually abused. This cannot be matched with Juliette's history since there is no evidence of sexual abuse of her as a young child until the episode of the sexual initiation with the mayor when she is 15 years old. But the prostitute wanting to dominate her clients, and Juliette also dominating other sexual partners, is a constant feature of the book. Sexual partners, notably 'Max F.', are treated as part-objects, there to satisfy her whims (p. 9). Juliette states repeatedly that she is excited by perversion (p. 64), a label which not uncontroversially she applies to herself as a 7- or 8-year-old to describe her own behaviour with her mother's 'friend' (p. 15). What we can note here is that Juliette, writing her story from her hospital bed, is given to self-blaming, including blaming herself as a 7- or 8-year-old child. This reinforces the confessional mode announced on the back cover. In her first sexual exchange with 'Max F.', she writes: 'Je le provoquais, j'établissais entre nous un lien pervers qui nous tiendrait à distance l'un de l'autre' (pp. 65–66) ('I provoked him, establishing between us a perverse rapport which would keep us apart from each other'). By the end of their relationship, he is ready to say to her that he is her dog, and she talks of having tamed him (pp. 78–79). This seems to confirm Welldon's theory: Juliette is setting up the relationship so that they cannot reach intimacy. According to Welldon, some of the aspects of the mother–infant relationship are reproduced in some forms of female prostitution: '[...] a splitting process is in full operation, together with a feeling of elation at being in complete control and in a dominant position in which revenge, conscious or unconscious, is the driving force' (p. 17). This certainly appears to be the case when Juliette sees herself as the actress Jane Fonda on the screen while pleasuring a client. Later, when she is studying political science in Paris, 'René V.', one of her lecturers, becomes her lover, and she describes their lovemaking as scenes she is playing in, with dialogues she is reciting, and René V. is totally submissive to her (p. 103). These examples seem to indicate a sense of narcissistic omnipotence in which Juliette is becoming her own spectacle.

According to Welldon, within the framework of perverse actions, women usually harm themselves while men carry out perverse actions on an outside object. It appears that Juliette carries out perversions on outside objects, namely men, while harming herself in the process. Kubie uses the expression 'making hate' for such actions (p. 33), where what is being expressed is nothing short of sadism, which Stoller defines as 'the erotic form of hatred' (p. 13). Welldon notes that very often, from being a 'victim' as a child, the adult becomes the 'victimiser', wanting to perpetrate on others the humiliation inflicted on them as children. In *Pourquoi moi?* there is no evidence of Juliette's having been humiliated as a child, except that the telling silence in the book is Juliette's experience of her father going to the Algerian war (first abandonment), and then being killed in action (second and lasting abandonment).

In many ways, this is the most important event in Juliette's psyche. Significantly she does not write about it, barely mentioning it (pp. 13–14).[19] According to Benjamin, the psychoanalytic theory of female development has not yet recognised the importance of the missing father.[20] What is likely is that her father's disappearance produced anger and infantile rage in her, as a healthy reaction, and perhaps also, at some level, guilt. Since we are informed that Juliette was born in 1957, in all probability she was around three years old when her father went to fight in the Algerian war. What Juliette also sees and experiences is her mother having been 'abandoned' by her husband. For most of her life, the mother will remain in solitude, living an austere life as a provincial primary school teacher. Juliette is determined that she will not follow in her mother's footsteps: '[…] elle a été piégée; sa vie, elle l'a passée avec une chaîne autour du cou' (p. 14) ('[…] she was trapped; her life has been spent with a chain round her neck'); further on, to describe their life together, she uses the powerful image of her mother choosing to bury them both alive in a village (p. 111). By contrast, Juliette is attracted by the philosophy of her grandmother, Émilie, who as a single mother raised her father, proved ferociously independent, and tells Juliette she will make something of her life as long as she does not tie herself down to a man.

If we bear in mind what happened to the young Juliette with her father 'disappearing', there is a possible correlation with Juliette's need to be in complete control of men so that they don't vanish again. Or, as on the occasion of one of her one-night stands, after the most daring intimate acts, she demands that a taxi be ordered straight away and then *she* vanishes. This behaviour is to be interpreted as Juliette regulating the timing and pacing of the exit. Using Winnicott's idea of destruction as a way of differentiating the self, Jessica Benjamin remarks:

> […] erotic domination expresses a basic differentiating tendency that has undergone a transformation. As we have seen, the fate of this tendency depends on whether it is met with the other's capitulation/retaliation or survival. The adult sadist, for example, is searching for a surviving other, but his search is already prejudiced by his childhood disappointment with an other who did not survive.[21]

Being dominant and regulating her sexual encounters will never make up for the childhood trauma of Juliette's father's death.[22] So there is an added dimension here which is the grief that Juliette is carrying.

One must not forget that behind Juliette's sexual perversions (in the psychoanalytical sense of the term) lie terror and anger, as Krout Tabin puts it: 'Sexuality thus becomes confused with terror and anger and, at the extreme of negativism, the inflicting of pain and taking complete control over the other. To control seems the opposite of engulfment.'[23] There is a glimpse of this phenomenon in the book when Juliette meets 'Max F.', and he dominates her throughout the night. Helping herself to his wallet in the morning (and leaving it out for him to see what she has done) is a gesture done as much for her own benefit, as a means of reassurance that she is still in control. Walking away into the sunshine, she says she feels she has escaped the worst by leaving his apartment, for she has felt so much pleasure that she fears becoming addicted to submission (p. 67). The main example, however, is when Juliette talks about the one man she fell in love with, 'Georges D.'. They were students together, and she tries to get him to notice her but it does not work. She then joins him in a café for a drink and engages in an intellectual debate about the presentation he has just made to the group. As this does not work either, she proposes bluntly to sleep with him: she is engaged in one-upmanship. In fact, all she wants is to sit next to him but, as she writes, she cannot afford to be ruled by her feelings, like her mother, faithful in her widow's status for all these years (p. 109). He rejects her offer in no uncertain terms, and she spends the next few days camped outside the school where he teaches, until his wife comes to talk to her and asks her to leave them alone. Juliette is then overcome by a sort of rage, taking out her anger with a phone call to her mother where she reproaches her for her upbringing.

What is significant in this relationship is the switch in Juliette from being in complete control to being totally dependent. And dependency brings with it the terror of annihilation which is exposed by Juliette being in love with 'Georges D.'. Juliette is trapped in an emotional binary system. Fear and control are part of the same issue. In this case, and judging by her behaviour, Juliette becomes the part-object of 'Georges D.'; in all the other cases, men are her part-objects. And yet, whether one is dominant or submissive in relationships, in neither situation is there real contact with the other.

What the study of perversion has shown is that beyond masculinist desires and sexualities are fears of dependency. Let us now turn to the situation of Juliette's diagnosis as HIV-positive to see what happens to her reading of desire as transgression and danger. First of all I need to give a few pointers which will help to contextualise the book in the history of the AIDS epidemic in France.

Published in 1987, the events narrated in *Pourquoi moi?* took place in 1985–1986. The fact that the narrator is a woman means that the cards are stacked against her. In a very lucid and pugilistic book, ACT-UP Paris (itself created only in 1989) broaches the question of women and the HIV virus.[24] According to them, the most forgotten woman in France in terms of prevention is not a prostitute, an African woman, a drug addict or a lesbian; it is 'Madame Tout-le-monde' (the average woman). The average woman is unlikely to come across any prevention advice of any kind since she does not go to any of the places where such advice is available.

Prevention in France only took off in 1987, as mentioned in the introduction. The first official campaign endorsed by the French government for the use of condoms was in 1987; too late for Juliette. Until 1987, only voluntary organisations such as VLS or AIDES and, at times and rather late in the day, the magazine *Gai Pied*[25] engaged in information and prevention.[26] Again, Juliette would have no particular reason to come across these or to go to the places where they were engaged in prevention. According to ACT-UP, lack of prevention is also linked to gender inequality, since in the early 1980s it was thought that AIDS could only be spread through 'high-risk groups' (homosexuals and drug addicts), and that heterosexual women were not particularly at risk. Hence very little research was being carried out on them. This message is reinforced by the book: Juliette is said to have contracted the HIV virus through sex with 'Pierre T.' who is bisexual; he is also supposed to have contaminated the woman who tells Juliette about him during the fateful phone call on Christmas day. There is actually no evidence to prove that this is the case (hence the text seems more a fiction than a testimonial account), especially given Juliette's sex life as narrated in the book, but the story that 'high-risk groups' are spreading the virus is perpetuated by presuppositions such as these. In 'Pierre T.'s bisexuality, it is presumably his homosexual side which puts him in the 'high-risk group' and which is therefore condemned, according to Juliette and by extension her readers.

Women who spoke about being HIV-positive were thought either to be drug addicts or to have had a lot of sexual partners. In any case they became stigmatised. Revealing one's HIV status was synonymous with social exclusion. Juliette knows that she cannot tell anyone about her HIV status, not even her friend and at times lover 'Kathleen B.', nor Henri who works with her (p. 121). Anne Souyris makes the point that because the French feminist movement had largely died down by the early 1980s, a woman's coming out as HIV-positive in France meant exclusion rather than identification with a community;[27] in short, there was nothing to be gained.

When Juliette is first diagnosed as being HIV-positive, she feels guilt:

> Je me suis dit: 'Tu n'as que ce que ce mérites'. Il me semblait entendre la voix de ma mère […] le monde avait un sens […] la morale était inscrite dans le ciel et […] on ne pouvait l'enfreindre sans périr. […]
> Et puis la révolte a été plus forte.
> Pourquoi moi? (pp. 134–35)

> I said to myself: 'You have what you deserve'. I thought I could hear my mother's voice. […] the world made sense […] a code of ethics was written in the sky, and […] if one transgressed it, it meant perdition. But then a sense of revolt took over.
> Why me?

The first thing that comes to Juliette's mind is the 'just punishment' narrative, but she is soon overcome by feelings of rebellion. The next thing she considers is the ultimate self-harm, amounting to self-destruction: suicide (pp. 122–23).[28] She opens the gas tap in her kitchen but, at the last minute, switches it off, overtaken by uncontrollable anger directed mostly towards men: '"Salauds, salauds, salauds." C'était les gens, les hommes, le monde, les autres' (p. 123) ('"Swine, swine, swine." It was people, men, the world, others'). She then rings an AIDS volunteer association, but is filled again by anger and says that she will not react like them by accepting her HIV status, adapting herself, and calmly waiting for death:

> Je me sentais sale, répugnante. Et j'avais envie d'en mettre partout, sur les murs comme ces gosses dégoûtants qui passent leurs doigts couverts de merde sur les rideaux et les murs. (pp. 123–24)

> I felt dirty, disgusting. And I wanted to spread it everywhere like those revolting kids who smear their fingers covered in shit on to curtains and walls.

Following on from that, she writes her script for the next day's radio programme, full of 'a sort of rage' (p. 124) – a significant emotional state which I will analyse later. She knows very well what is at stake the first time she has to pick herself up to do her job: 'Il me fallait écrire ma chronique. Si je ne l'écrivais pas aujourd'hui, je n'en écrirais plus jamais' (p. 121) ('I had to write my review. If I didn't write it today, I would never write another one'). In this sentence, one can feel how close Juliette is to fragmenting. Over the next few days, it appears that a splitting process is continuing to operate, confirming Thomé-Renault's study in *Le Traumatisme de la mort annoncée*, in which she refers to the professional hyperactivity that some HIV-positive people (understandably) go into in order to keep anguish at bay.[29]

Next, the symbolic spreading of dirt takes place. Her topic is the corruption of left-wing politicians who look like angels. Her producer, on listening to the recording, calls her 'diabolical', which brings the following remark from her: 'Il ne croyait pas si bien dire' (p. 124) ('He didn't know he had hit the nail on the head'). This is significant, since Juliette is now constructing herself as a source of evil, as a disciple of the devil, with its association with death. One can see yet again the influence of Catholicism in France. On learning that she is HIV-positive, Juliette writes, '[…] j'étais pourrie, je portais le mal en moi' (p. 120) ('[…] I was rotten, I was carrying wickedness in me'). It is as if, feeling that she is carrying wickedness inside, she is acting devilishly on the outside.

The other important factor is that, as I highlighted earlier, she describes herself writing her script full of 'a sort of rage' (p. 124). The fact that she uses this expression (which she will repeat a number of times throughout the last part of the book to describe her inner state) is significant, for in the reaction in which she compares spreading the virus to a child's spreading excrement on to walls and curtains, one can almost feel the child's pain associated with her father's leaving, a pain reawakened by the diagnosis. Now her world is crumbling once more. Now she is reverting to the same reflex action as then. It is as if she is actually sign-posting her own infection, through having put herself in situations where she was at risk (though she appears to genuinely believe that she was *not* at risk), as if unable to escape the emotional place she was in when her father vanished. There is, however, another interpretation of her reaction. Juliette is also combating representations of HIV-positive people as victims, the representation of an 'AIDS sufferer' which totally and purposefully disempowers PWAs.

In order to try and gain some deeper understanding of Juliette's emotional state, I will consider once again the question of masculinist desires and sexualities, this time within the framework of Juliette's diagnosis. The day after her diagnosis, Juliette picks up a businessman in a hotel, has unprotected sex with him, and then with the taxi driver who is taking her home, feeling when she collapses into her bed in the early hours that she no longer has the virus since she has passed it on to them. As when she acted as a prostitute, although this time she is not accepting money for sex, Juliette appears to be splitting again. As we saw, Welldon writes that being in control and in a dominant position are linked to wanting to take revenge (p. 17) which appears to be the case here. After a lull, Juliette reappropriates for herself active desire as a sexualised woman in the weeks following her diagnosis. She has as much sex as possible, with as many men as possible, usually as a one-off encounter, and always without any form of protection whatsoever (pp. 185–86), despite her doctor's warnings that she should use a condom at all times. In so doing, she reinvents herself as a seductive witch ('Je devenais une sorte de sorcière séduisante', p. 186), an avenger for women, including her mother (p. 156). But what is she avenging her mother for, if not the death of her father and her subsequent life as a widow? Juliette is getting her own back for having been let down by men, and above all for having been an exploited sexual object. She is playing men's game and beating them at it. For example, 'Michel B.', the director of the radio station, is under pressure to take her off her programme once she has blown the whistle on one of the media magnates whom she holds responsible for the death of her friend and ex-lover 'Kathleen B.'; in her job, too, she has turned into an avenger. But he uses his position to extract from her a much-awaited 'dirty weekend' in Portugal, under the excuse of having to discuss her future. They have a lot of unprotected sex. Juliette is being irresponsible in not using condoms, hurting men by doing what they do, and mirroring what she sees as her contamination. She is playing on their sense of promiscuity and ensnaring them, mirroring her own trap.

There is, however, a double-bind in place. According to Jaccomard, representations of women in AIDS writing in France centre on the image of the dangerous witch or of the admired and glorified woman who is totally powerless.[30] Juliette seems to fall into the former category, describing herself as a seductive witch, an image associated with strong and independent women, whose male equivalent over the centuries is the stereotype of the mercenary. In terms of myths, these representations of women provide a mirror image to those of the male PWA, represented either as angel or demon (Hélène refers to the person who contaminated Martin as the Devil as we saw in Chapter 1; Hervé Guibert was often portrayed as an angel, albeit a fallen one).[31] Juliette equally enters into the representations of HIV-positive people as murderers, denounced by ACT-UP Paris.[32] Refusing to be the victim, she becomes the perpetrator. Juliette on the loose in Paris infecting as many men as possible could also play into male fantasies as the epitome of the rifle-woman (*Flintenweiber*), and by extension the castrating woman, as analysed by Klaus Theweleit in his book about male fantasies.[33] This echoes Juliette's own fantasies as a student when she identifies with Jane Fonda in *Klute* as a warrior, an outlaw, who occasionally prostitutes herself but is never compromised by a man (p. 57). The very fact that her identity is limited to a first name contributes to the association with prostitution, since as Theweleit points out, 'Women who have only first names are somehow on offer to the public; whether movie stars or servants, they are somehow prostitutes'.[34] These remarks resonate with earlier reflections prompted by the episode of Juliette's sexual initiation with the mayor. *Pourquoi moi?* has echoes of a soft porn novel exploiting male fantasies which makes its contribution as a representation of women's AIDS experience questionable. Though the book is presented as a confession (in itself a well-rehearsed title for soft porn: *Confessions of a young girl*, etc.), the latter part of the text matches the description of a revenge narrative, like Winer's book discussed in Chapter 3. This thriller aspect mirrors what Weeks calls the moral panic of the AIDS crisis from 1983 to 1986, which lasted until 1987 in France. Hence the genre of the book matches and captures the mood of the time.

But Juliette is not simply a perpetrator. She is also given to self-harm, at risk of increasing her viral load with such an active sex life, or of getting a different strain of the HIV virus; we now also know that people can pass on to each other strains of drug-resistant HIV. As the following telling sentence seems to confirm, unprotected sex could also symbolise the fact that she never felt protected emotionally as a child, and later as a teenager, against the predatory and insatiable sexual appetite of the mayor and other so-called powerful men she encountered in her career in the media and in her dealings with politicians. While she is deliberating whether to have unprotected sex or not, she exclaims, 'Qui m'avait protégée, moi?' (p. 132) ('Who had protected me?').

I mentioned above the terror and anger at the root of Juliette's sexual perversions. It is undeniable that Juliette is angry with men; she states quite categorically near the end of the book that she has no regrets about having had unprotected sex with any of these men (p. 191). She is running away, launching herself into frenzied activities in order to keep anguish at bay. My contention is that Juliette is also angry with herself for having bought in to men's masculinist desires, for having acted out sexuality as performance, for having been wild and irresponsible, and for having read transgression and desire as without consequences. At one stage she uses 'we' to describe men who see themselves as immortal, with their thirst for power and fame which she points out she has also tasted (p. 190); Juliette has mirrored men's desire for omnipotence, signing her own self-destruction.

Eventually, Juliette develops illnesses which put her medically into the category of people with AIDS. She has to be hospitalised. There is a very marked change of tone in the book, which starts to read like a confession. Juliette suddenly finds that two of the men she has known for a long time are willing to be there for her and to meet her needs, despite knowing the 'truth' about her HIV status – one was a student with her at university called Jean-Jacques and the other one is Henry, her colleague and one of her ex-sexual partners. She says she has the impression that she is discovering him (p. 193). For the first time, she is acknowledging her own needs, and is surprised that he is there for her. A lifetime script is being rewritten: some men can meet her needs. Her anger seems to vanish, and she decides to start writing her story after meeting Jean-Jacques again. The creative process is linked to a new sense of self, Juliette describing each word she puts on paper as tearing away from herself an old shell, a crust, which reveals a fragile skin finally smooth and healed (p. 212). This metaphor shows the new strength gained by Juliette after having achieved a new sense of self. Now her only regret is to have judged some men like Henry too harshly, and not to have dared to love Georges. In the last paragraph of the book, she says that she is not a witch, and that it is not the devil nor a God righting a wrong that has condemned her, but a virus. *Pourquoi moi?* seems to change genres, from a soft porn text playing on male fantasies to a revenge narrative in the thriller tradition, and finally to a confession.

'Confession' smacks of a religious conversion but it may be that the publishers felt it necessary to give the book such a label in order to help readers accept what they describe as a 'crude' experience. It is only if Juliette is repentant that her story becomes palatable, otherwise her account reads too subversively for the hegemonic order. This was also the reaction of the first readers of the manuscript, presumably for the publisher, who are reported to have been shocked by Juliette's story, and to have feared that HIV-positive readers of both sexes would start in turn to contaminate sexual partners (p. 214).

If Laygues' book was labelled a 'testimony', why is Juliette's labelled a 'confession'? When one speaks, one is not only taking up a position as subject in a discourse but one is also *subjected* to the rules and regulations of this discourse. As Foucault has shown in *The History of Sexuality*, 'the confessional mode, developed within Catholicism, is the form which [...] power often takes'.[35] It is 'an effect of spiritual reconversion'[36] in which the reader becomes the authority figure, with the power to absolve the repentant sinner. Foucault claims that the relations of power between the person in authority (in this case the reader) and the sinner 'have subsequently been transferred to other more recent discourses which often utilize the confessional mode *to define and constitute sexuality*' (my emphasis).[37]

According to what is written on the back cover, the 'lesson' to be learned from reading *Pourquoi moi?* is that the extent of this illness ('cette maladie') puts in jeopardy sexual freedom; the implication is that if you are an 'unattached, young and ambitious female journalist', there is some logic in your contracting AIDS. Yet again, the 'just punishment' discourse resurfaces, but this time the three adjectives attached to it broaden the spectrum of repression from sexual orienta-tion to defining women's roles (young women should be married and not too ambitious). 'Particular discourses set parameters through which desire is produced, regulated and channelled.'[38] The discourse on the back cover of this book is nothing less than an attempt to patrol sexual-ity, and especially to 'save' monogamous heterosexual women from the 'dangers' of same-sex sexuality or non-monogamous relationships, and also to obliquely reinforce the role of women as procreators. The enemy is seen as 'Pierre T.' because he was bisexual, and therefore it is his homosexual side which is 'condemned'. But, and this is where the three genres of the soft porn novel, the revenge narrative and the confession conflate, the lesson is also addressed to men who should be wary of women wanting sex, for these could actually be like Juliette and infect them with the HIV virus. There is no doubt that the account of Juliette's sexual adventures could be arousing to heterosexual men; this is certainly not the effect when she ends up with a death sentence in her hospital bed. The implications from the revenge narrative are that some of her male sexual partners are likely to have been infected too; everyone gets their 'just punishment'. Unlike the case of Martin in Laygues' book, it is women's sexualities that are on trial. At the heart of French society is the idea of women as mothers, with the implication that on their reproductive powers depends the future generation of the nation-state. Juliette's story is framed as a confession to promote that idea, illustrating once more the proposition that Catholicism is an important determinant of French constructions of the nationality/ sexuality relationship. It is no coincidence that the 'lesson' to readers in *Pourquoi moi?* echoes the lesson in *Sida, Témoignage sur la vie et la mort de Martin*, and it shows the power of forces of repression in French AIDS writings of the 1980s.

3 Winer: Masculinity, Grief and Sexuality

Published in 1988, *Bienvenue dans le monde du Sida!* (*Welcome to the World of AIDS!*) claims that it is an 'histoire vécue' ('a real life/true story').[1] The back cover tells us that a woman called Mona sleeps with men after meeting them in nightclubs. In the morning, she leaves a message with her red lipstick on the bathroom mirror, always the same one. One cannot help but draw the conclusion that the message is the actual title of the book, especially since a red lipstick lies below the handwritten title on the front cover. The blurb then introduces Mike Winer, a 23-year-old investigative journalist for a Los Angeles newspaper. He is engaged and his fiancée is expecting their child. One night he meets his fate in a hotel room. The text then reads: 'Il ne sait pas encore qu'il est mort. Mort pour quelques minutes de jouissance.' ('He does not know yet that he is dead. Dead for a few minutes of pleasure.')

I will start by summing up the story. The book has a first-person narrator identifying himself as the author, Mike Winer. In Chapter 1, the narrator tells us that, while still a trainee journalist, he is put in charge of an investigation concerning drugs and prostitution. This section ends with a reflection that foresees the dangers to come; we realise that this is a flashback narrative. There are very seldom any dates in this narrative, nor a strict chronology. It is therefore difficult to situate events, except for the year, 1986. In Chapter 3, the narrator has unprotected sex with Mona Hessler, and as readers we have in mind the plot announced on the back cover, though the narrator is unaware of his fate, especially since Mona does not leave a message on the bathroom mirror. Winer learns that Karine Wooley, his fiancée, is pregnant, having stopped taking the pill without telling him. For the purpose of his investigation, Winer meets Bert Coffman, an HIV-positive man. The latter describes the woman who gave him the virus, and says that before leaving the next morning she wrote 'Welcome to the World of AIDS!' on the bathroom mirror. Again, the reader is aware that her description matches that of the woman Winer has just had unprotected sex with, but Winer seems oblivious to this. Through-out the following chapters, references to the narrator's feeling unwell and being feverish, as well as to other symptoms he displays (for example, pp. 39, 88), suggest the immuno-suppressant effect of the HIV virus on the body, but Winer appears oblivious to any warning signs, driven by his investigation and its deadline. So there is a degree of awareness on the part of the reader who knows more than the narrator telling the story; this ironic effect will be repeated throughout the book. The world Winer enters for his investigation is extremely dangerous; Linda, the prostitute he interviews, is killed, the murder being disguised as suicide, but an anonymous phone call tips him off. He is up against figures in organised crime, possibly the Mafia, who do not want any publicity linking AIDS and prostitution, especially as business is already declining. After a verbal warning delivered by two burly gentlemen and ignored by Winer, his flat is ransacked and all his research material taken. He carries on with his investigation and is severely beaten up, before discovering that there is a contract out on him.

His relationship with Karine is really peripheral to the story. She spends most of her time with her mother away from Los Angeles, and they speak occasionally on the phone. She comes to see him twice, but the third time he puts her off, and his relationship with her does not stop him from sleeping around. Meanwhile, he is gradually being accepted by the Wooley family, going to their home for Sunday lunch. In parallel to this, Winer is struggling with his declining health, apparently oblivious to any warning signs.

Suddenly, after 118 pages, he realises that Mona Hessler fits the description of the woman who contaminated Bert Coffman and who before leaving the next morning wrote 'Welcome to the World of AIDS!' on the bathroom mirror. He tries to track her down, and eventually succeeds. She does not know Bert Coffman, but in view of Winer's telling her that he is likely to have an AIDS test because of recent illnesses, she decides to contact the sexual partners she met after sleeping with Winer and to warn them about AIDS. She thinks Winer may have contaminated her. She is shot at by one of her ex-partners who has become HIV-positive and believes that *she* has given him the virus. Meanwhile, Winer is more and more convinced that he has AIDS, and he even tells his friend Ted without having the diagnosis confirmed (p. 152). His health is badly deteriorating, especially his spine which is in danger of rupturing, and he has to be admitted to hospital, where he speaks at one point of spending three months (p. 178). In fact, he never leaves hospital. He is under the care of Dr Aaron Burr who is the Wooleys' family doctor. It becomes clear that the whole story has been written in hospital where Winer has asked for three notebooks (p. 182), and started by writing down the title of his story: 'La mort pour une minute de jouissance' (p. 188) ('Death for one minute of pleasure'). He only finds out officially that he is HIV-positive on page 188, and the book finishes nine pages later. He is told by the doctor that Mona Hessler is also HIV-positive and that she has probably contaminated him (this is so implausible a detail that it contributes to the belief that this is a work of fiction despite its label of a 'true story'). The last few pages narrate Winer's rapid decline; he is diagnosed as having bone cancer. He writes frantically to try and finish his story. He informs his future father-in-law that he is HIV-positive, letting the older man tell his daughter. She turns out to be HIV-positive also and decides not to have anything to do with him, but to keep the child. Winer is completely alone, except for the medical staff.

The last line that he writes is 'Demain, je reprendrai la suite de mon récit' (p. 197) ('Tomorrow, I will carry on with my story').

Mike Winer's book could presumably have been written in English as the text invites us to believe;[2] it is set in the United States. All names and places have been changed so that people could not be identified but Winer felt that they could still be traced so he insisted that the book should be published in French and in France, as a further precaution (p. 195). If the book was originally written in English, there is an issue as to who translated it, which remains unclear and unacknowledged. If we are to believe the text, Dr Burr — who looked after Winer when he was ill — had been asked by the latter that, if anything should happen to him, he should send his three notebooks to Winer's friends in France. These friends are themselves writers living on the 'Côte d'Azur' and they will tidy up the manuscript (p. 195); I have no way of checking whether this happened and, if so, to what extent. In a sense, the place of publication tallies with this account since the book was published by a Monaco-based publisher. There appear to be only two editorial interventions in the text, although the usual convention 'N.d.E.' ('editor's note') is not respected. On page 41, a footnote 'authenticates' the narrator's account of interviewing a murderer, giving the murderer's 'real' name, as opposed to the fictional one invented in the story. On the last page of the book, a sentence introduces a paragraph in italics and explains its origin; it is a note by Dr Burr which was sent in the envelope with the three notebooks from Winer. Dr Burr's note states that Mike Winer died six days after writing the last line of his story. Dr Burr admits they had lied to him by telling him he had one or two months left (p. 195). In fact, the medical team had been expecting him to die for more than a week; he weighed only forty kilos. Dr Burr goes on to say that he is sending the manuscript as promised, and in order to finish Winer's story, he adds that Karine Wooley gave birth to a boy who tested HIV-negative. Offset from Dr Burr's paragraph one reads: 'Ici s'achève l'histoire tragique de Mike Winer' ('Here ends the tragic story of Mike Winer'), the very last line of the book, which gives the impression that it is written by his two friends, or by the editor. Since death interrupts the book, as a reader, I am aware of Chambers's argument that the reader feels an obligation 'to continue the work of witness […] it requires realization',[3] and that 'I am dying' only comes to *signify* 'I am dead' with the act of reading.[4] In this case, as reader I actively participate both in the narrative and in the act of writing death by reading it.

Having given a lengthy résumé of the book, I would like to proceed by examining whether it tallies with what we are led to expect by the title and the back cover blurb. Billed as some sort of thriller, with the woman as the killer and the man as the victim, as the book unfolds, it reads more like Mike Winer narrating the story of what has happened to him (though these two story lines are not incompatible). When the first-person narrator realises that he could also have been the victim of the woman known as Mona Hessler, 118 pages have elapsed, and this story line recedes into the background in the second half of the book. No genre is specified in the book other than 'true/real life story' on the front cover which would, as in the case of Laygues' book, give the impression that it is a testimony.[5] The identity of the narrative voice should not be taken for granted. We know that Mike Winer is not the name of the real 'author'. According to Michel Danthe who enquired with the publisher, a pseudonym was used but the book's narrative is based on a 'true story'.[6] As we saw, there is, throughout the text, an ironic distance between the first-person narrator and the reader who is aware of aspects that the narrator does not seem to recognise. But the story in itself sounds much more like fiction than veridicality (in Walkerdine's sense of the word – see introduction). It is almost as if the reader is invited inside the text with his/her own version of events, which supersedes at times an erroneous version from the narrative voice. This creates various regimes of truth which, while cancelling each other out, build an overall sense that the story is fiction.

It seems quite probable that Mike Winer wanted the title of his book to be 'La mort pour une minute de jouissance' (p. 188) ('Death for one minute of pleasure'). Although this phrase is repeated almost verbatim in the last line of the back cover blurb, one can only speculate that either Winer's friends, or more probably his publisher, saw the story of the woman spreading AIDS as the main selling point of the book, and transformed it into some kind of a thriller, especially with the glossy front cover design. This situates the book within the tradition of a revenge narrative and echoes some aspects of Juliette's book; it also reinforces representations of AIDS narratives as detective stories.[7] It is no coincidence that these two significant books dealing with AIDS, published in France within a year of each other, should cast women as avengers. There is no doubt that the 'moral panic' period of the AIDS pandemic which lasted from 1983 to 1987 in France is reflected here in the choice of the thriller genre. The theory behind this marketing strategy could well have been that if the book captured the mood of the time and tapped into a collective 'hysteria', then it would sell. Ideologically, Williamson shows how the narrative of horror (which often has a detective story as an antidote or counter-plot) is used in AIDS stories, as the Gothic was used in the eighteenth and nineteenth centuries where 'demons and monsters threaten the innocent, and nature – including human nature – is constantly fearsome'.[8] Like Juliette, Mona Hessler is the dangerous witch, the 'avenger'. Again, as in the books considered in the previous two chapters, this confirms Jaccomard's thesis that representations of women in AIDS writing in France centre around the image of the dangerous witch or the admired and glorified woman who is totally powerless;[9] women are either killers, if they are engaged in *active* sexuality (Mona Hessler), or *passive* victims (Karine Wooley). Mona Hessler also reflects representations of HIV-positive people as murderers, representations that were denounced by ACT-UP Paris,[10] and on which the extreme right in France played to suggest that HIV-positive people should all be locked up in 'sidatoria'.[11] Mona on the loose in Los Angeles infecting as many men as possible could also play into male fantasies as the epitome of the rifle-women (*Flintenweiber*), and by extension the castrating woman, according to Klaus Theweleit's analysis in his book about male fantasies;[12] hence some of the appeal of the book has echoes of the soft porn tone of *Pourquoi moi?* What is also striking in these two books is that a hetero-sexual woman who constructs herself as an *active* rather than a *passive* agent in negotiating her own sexuality is dangerous, a witch, a cause of death. There are no positive images of homosexual people, nor of prostitutes or drug addicts in the book. Prostitutes and drug addicts are mostly dismissed as junkies. Gay sex is alluded to once by the narrator when he is interviewing someone in a gay bar, and he writes that the back-room practices which he *imagines* go on make his hair stand on end (p. 73).

Within the archaeology of AIDS writing in France, the following seems clear. The publisher's wish to emphasise the story line of the woman contaminating men, especially in the title, is in effect a way of controlling human sexuality. If the back cover message of *Pourquoi moi?* states unmistakably that there is a certain inevitability about an 'unattached, young and ambitious female journalist' catching AIDS (hence, women should not seek independence and freedom to assert themselves outside of marriage, professionally and sexually) – and also serves as a warning to young men not to have sex with them – the message in *Bienvenue dans le monde du Sida!* is a warning to young people that Pleasure = Death. So the discourse from both publishers is almost evangelical. They assert their own power in the discursive field of sexualities. Their message is aimed at regulating and disciplining women's and, by implication, men's desire.

The book reflects a specific time in the epidemic, 1986. Since the story was presumably written in the United States, it is worth noting that in America, by May 1987, 20,489 people had already died from AIDS-related illnesses, and there were 36,058 cases.[13] This of course does not account for all the people who were carrying the virus but were not counted in the statistics. In the book, the virus is described as an enemy which, thanks to its disguise, tricks the border police (the T4 cells) and invades our territory (p. 76); this description is very close to that of Alain Emmanuel Dreuilhe in *Corps à corps* (see Chapter 5). Most people only knew that they were HIV-positive when they started to develop opportunistic illnesses. By then a substantial majority saw their health decline rapidly because their CD counts had dropped too much for their immune system to work satisfactorily. Hence for the characters in *Bienvenue dans le monde du Sida!*, having AIDS is synonymous with being condemned to die (p. 42).[14] This also explains the back cover text, 'Dead for a few minutes of pleasure', which is a very puritanical statement in a time of moral panic and repression.

Bienvenue dans le monde du Sida! is the first book to claim to have been written by a heterosexual man who has contracted the HIV virus through heterosexual sex. Hence in terms of Weeks's periodisation, we are entering the third phase, in which it became clear that AIDS was not simply a homosexual disease. At the time, the illness was associated with drug addicts exchanging needles and with gay sexuality (p. 60). Hence, anyone trying to negotiate safe sex with their sexual partner often found the other person disappearing on suspicion that they had the virus (p. 46). In the case of prostitutes, clients still insisted on not using condoms, as in the pre-AIDS era (p. 88). No wonder Winer finds it difficult during his investigation to get homosexuals to agree to be interviewed; they feared retribution (p. 66). Heterosexual people often believed that the 'gay plague' as it was known was unlikely to affect them: there was a great deal of heterosexual complacency about the illness, as demonstrated by Winer's attitude.

We have seen that the story, presented within the thriller convention of *whodunnit?*, modified into *who contaminated whom?*, is in fact more the story of Winer's life. The answer to the question *who contaminated whom?* is clearly implied by the cover of the book, but when we look at the actual evidence from the text, it is far from clear-cut. First of all, Mike Winer could have been HIV-positive and asymptomatic for a few years (and that is the most likely scenario given his sexual history). Secondly, there is no evidence to suggest that the story related by Bert Coffman about a woman avenger who writes the message used as the title of the book on a bathroom mirror is in fact true (bearing in mind that when I use the word 'truth' I understand it to be 'a material, discursive, political and subjective question');[15] Winer never gets this story confirmed. Thirdly, as Mona Hessler herself suspects when Winer contacts her again, *he* could have been the person who contaminated her (p. 139). Finally, when Winer's doctor announces to him that he is HIV-positive and tells him that Mona Hessler is also HIV-positive and that it seems that she has contaminated him unknowingly (p. 188), there is absolutely no shred of evidence

72

to support this scenario as opposed to the opposite one (and it points yet again to the text being a work of fiction rather than a 'true story').

In fact, *who contaminated whom?* is not an issue. But since we are within the framework of the thriller genre, the question of *whodunnit?* is relevant: my main intention is to interpret the book as playing on different readings of 'death'. I would argue that Winer has long been emotionally dead. Because of his personal traumatic history, and his investment in traditional heterosexual desire, Mike Winer in a sense has signed his own death warrant. His response to his personal history is highly gendered.

I want to focus my critical intervention on an event in Mike Winer's life so important in my eyes that I missed it on first reading![16] As he introduces himself in Chapter 1, the narrator states that he comes from a modest background and that he was orphaned aged 16 when his parents and his younger sister were killed in a car crash, remarking that he has made himself what he is on his own. The only sharing of his feelings about this event in the whole book is this sentence: 'Pour être franc avec moi-même, je dois admettre que ce difficile départ dans la vie a laissé en moi des traces profondes, indélébiles' (p. 13) ('To be honest with myself, I must admit that this difficult start in life has left a deep and indelible mark on me').

In *Men and Grief*,[17] Carol Staudacher, having made the initial point that grief is gendered, talks about men's various grief 'responses'. Two of these categories seem to apply to Mike Winer; risk-taking and excessive sexual activity. Risk-taking is often 'a thinly disguised desire for self-destruction'.[18] Excessive sexual activity is a way to numb the pain of loss (and in the case of Winer, *losses*) rather than to acknowledge it. Staudacher argues that a man thinks he will 'remain less vulnerable if he concerns himself with physical release and performance'.[19] A consequence of this behaviour is that all sorts of other emotions, including fear, will not be expressed and the man is much less likely 'to exhibit genuine compassion towards others'.[20] From a psychoanalytical point of view, Melanie Klein, in her writings on 'Mourning and Manic-Depressive States',[21] points to the pitfalls of not experiencing mourning: 'Emotions in general become more inhibited;

in other cases it is mainly feelings of love which become stifled [...]'.[22] These comments read like a blueprint for *Bienvenue dans le monde du Sida!* I have of course no way of knowing if Mike Winer did grieve for the loss of his parents and his younger sister, or if these events happened. But viewed from the perspective of the text, this psycho-analytical theory makes a lot of sense.

If we deal first of all with the issue of risk-taking, the narrator conducts an investigation into the world of drugs and prostitution. Bearing in mind that we are in 1986, he soon encounters prostitutes, junkies and homosexuals who have AIDS. When he enters the world of prostitution, he is faced with pimps, acting either for a syndicate or the Mafia, who threaten his life. Because of the AIDS scare, business is poor but rich clients still want to have unprotected sex, no doubt because if they pay they want to have total control, but also because of the thrill associated with their own risk-taking. The last thing the people running the business want is a lengthy article in one of the main papers associating AIDS with unprotected sex with a prostitute. But the narrator perseveres with his enquiries. His flat is turned inside out and all his research material taken. The prostitute who had agreed to talk to him is killed, and her murder covered up as suicide; he is savagely beaten up, learning a few days later that he has almost lost his sight in one eye because of the savagery of the attack. Still, he does not give up, showing no visible sign(s) of fear, confirming Staudacher's analysis above. The police inspector who links the death of the prosti-tute with Mike's visit to her shortly before she was killed discovers eventually that there is a contract out on him, but by then he is dying from bone cancer, one of the consequences of the HIV virus. What is remarkable throughout this whole history of threats is that Winer acts as if he is unaffected by them. At no point does he consider giving up his investigation, either for his own sake or because he is engaged and his future wife is expecting his child. It is as if he has no fear, or rather as if he is not in touch with any fear, confirming the analysis of Klein and Staudacher.

Secondly, exploring the domain of sexualities, Winer makes it plain that he likes to have one-night stands involving unprotected sex, and this continues even when he is engaged to Karine. His routine is to go to a nightclub called Sammy's where he drinks and smokes dope before ending up in bed with a different woman every time. His high-risk sexual behaviour means that he is almost sign-posting his own road to becoming infected by HIV. By the time he wakes up the next morning, he is usually wondering how he has ended up in the hotel room he is lying in (p. 25). The sexual experience is not one of intimacy. When his fiancée rings him after the night and morning he has spent having sex with Mona Hessler, he frantically gets hold of some poppers in order to perform with Karine when Mona has only just left his room. Sexual performance is the only thing that seems to count for him, when his body is telling him that he needs to rest. Performance is a mask for anxiety and vulnerability. Performance stands between him and any possibility of intimacy with Karine. He talks quite openly about his future with Karine and says that she will probably be frigid by the time she is forty, and that he will have one or more mistresses. His sexual appetite will have to be satisfied at the expense of intimacy with Karine. He is already projecting in the future that he will be sustaining his sexual behaviour, as a proof/guarantee of his masculinity.

The exact expression he uses to describe Sammy's is 'ce lieu de débauche et de perdition où je me damne avec délectation […]' (p. 17) ('this place of debauchery and perdition where I damn myself with delight […]'). 'Damner' carries the idea of condemnation, and, in Catholic terms, of hell. There is a real drive within him to press the self-destruct button on the road to 'jouissance'. Because Mike Winer only ever practises unprotected sex despite the risks he is made aware of in all the interviews he is conducting for his enquiry, his excessive sexual activity is to be seen in the context of risk-taking, further defined in what Staudacher describes as self-destruction. Because of his investigation, he is ideally placed through interviewing prostitutes, junkies and homosexuals as well as some doctors (pp. 65–66) to be aware of the spreading HIV virus, and of the need to use condoms. He can write in this context, '[…] les jeunes ne sont absolument pas conscients du danger qui les menace' (p. 53) ('[…] young people are totally oblivious to the dangers threatening them') without relating this to his own sexual behaviour. This confirms the research done by Kimmel and Levine who state in the context of their article on 'Men and *AIDS*', 'It appears that a significant number of men continue to engage in high risk behavior, even though they know better.'[23] There is a collusion between Winer's dissociation, due to his being out of touch with his emotions, itself rooted in his gendered grief response, and a risk-taking element grounded in predatory sex as a form of hetero-sexual masculine potency.[24] The one dream recounted in the book shows clearly that my interpretation has some mileage in it. Winer says that he falls asleep and dreams of sunny coves, of windsurfing. He is swimming like a fish towards Mona Hessler who is on a deserted raft, lost, one hundred metres from the beach (p. 175). The sexual imagery is powerful: sun, sea, sand, and water where he swims in his element. He derives some of his pleasure from 'rescuing' the lost woman, hence there is an element of danger associated with his thrill. But the risk-taking is calculated; they are only one hundred metres from the beach. Still, if the beach represents safety and conventional society, Winer needs to deviate from the norm in order to feel the sexual buzz (as his regular visits to Sammy's show). The end result is the same; he is emotionally dead, and therefore damns himself.

In the book Winer talks about 'Death for one minute of pleasure', linking sexuality with death. And yet, as we saw above, his own death is almost sign-posted by himself. In many ways, he is already emotion-ally dead long before he contracts the HIV virus, probably since the unresolved grief episode. The sexual behaviour he adopts puts himself and others at risk of getting infected. And if he is not killed by illnesses he is likely to be the victim of a contract killing because of his investigation in the world of prostitution. Hence he approaches his job with the same element of risk-taking. The fact that he is led to believe that he was infected by Mona Hessler is not relevant. In fact, as I mentioned above, he could have been HIV-positive for several years before getting any symptoms. Once again the analysis by Klein and Staudacher is pertinent. Feelings, especially fear, appear to be difficult for Winer to access. He seems to be on a collision course with self-destruction.

When he learned about doing masculinities, Winer picked up the myth of the invincible man, which does not serve him well when he starts to be ill since he simply ignores his symptoms. As he writes, '[…] la moindre atteinte à mon intégrité physique me révolte …' (p. 71) ('[…] the slightest dent in my physical integrity makes me mad…'); in other words, the knight cannot have any chinks in his armour, his body cannot let him down. Likewise, a man never cries – despite terrific pain – 'J'en pleurerais si je n'étais un homme …' (p. 176) ('I would cry if I weren't a man …').

There are remarkable parallels between the character of Mike Winer and that of Juliette in *Pourquoi moi?* This is no coincidence since they have both adopted the values of traditional heterosexual masculinities, starting with the myth of the invincible man. Winer says openly that he never thought about the possibility of getting AIDS: 'Cela n'arrive qu'aux autres' (p. 16) ('It only happens to other people'); we saw in Chapter 2 that a leitmotiv for Juliette right from her childhood was 'It won't happen to me.' In addition, there is a great deal of heterosexual complacency in these remarks; AIDS is viewed as the 'gay plague'. Mike is really scathing about his friend Philip who, according to him, leads a boring life, being in love with his partner and not straying; he feels that Philip is simply Charlotte's double (p. 16). Heterosexual adventurous performance is defined against 'boring' predictable monogamy. In fact, on one occasion, he tries to get Philip drunk and to go to Sammy's with the declared intention of getting him to have a one-night stand; he also admits that once he made a pass at Philip's partner, Charlotte (pp. 16–20). Juliette talks in similar terms about her mother and resents her boring life; she is described as having lived her life with a chain around her neck. Winer says that he would prefer to die at 50 with his lifestyle than live until 80 the kind of mediocre life Philip is likely to lead (p. 20); Juliette also feels strongly that she does not want to end up trapped like her mother. There is something really unsettling for both of them and for their own subjectivity about the lives of others who appear to them to have compromised. They both want to claim the thrill of dangerous risk-taking, as if it is the only way of 'feeling' alive.

It is not only self-destruction but also the destruction of others that is at stake in this story. Based on the evidence of the text, Winer is likely to have infected his fiancée Karine, who could in turn pass on the virus to the unborn baby. And yet when it dawns on him (after a jocular remark from Dr Burr who says that he will tell him what is wrong with him, even if it is AIDS) that all his symptoms point to his being HIV-positive (pp. 117–18), it is only after trying to trace Mona Hessler whom he suspects has given him the virus that he thinks of them. With no chronology in the book, it is difficult to gauge how much time has elapsed. But he himself reflects, 'Pour la première fois, je pense à Karine!' (p. 139) ('For the first time, I think of Karine!'), twenty-two pages later. This manifestation of his behaviour makes me want to revisit his relationship with Karine in the context of men who are not able to grieve being much less likely 'to exhibit genuine compassion towards others'.[25] 'Emotions in general become more inhibited; in other cases it is mainly feelings of love which become stifled [...].'[26]

The least one can say is that Winer does not seem to show any compassion for Karine, especially when he lets Mr Wooley announce to his daughter that he, Mike, is HIV-positive. On learning that she has been tested and is positive, he does not try to contact her and never speaks to her again (p. 191). And this lack of compassion is repeated throughout the history of their relationship. He is also very open from the outset about not being in love with her, making it plain that he is interested in social climbing, and in her family fortune (pp. 13, 15). He describes her sexual performance as conscientious and laborious, before adding that getting her to reach an orgasm is hell (p. 16). Winer is using his own sexual yardstick to assess Karine's worth. Money and sexual performance is what she is judged on. She passes one test (thanks to her father) but not the other. It is also worth noting that he uses the phrase 'pour lui faire prendre son plaisir' ('to make her reach an orgasm'), which constructs him as an active agent, and her as a passive recipient; *he* is responsible for her orgasm. After he has spent a night of drugs, alcohol and casual sex, with Mona Hessler in fact as it will later fatefully turn out, Karine bursts into his flat, blossoming and spontaneously affectionate with him (p. 31). She tells him that she misses him, and he writes, 'Si je l'aimais, ce serait vraiment merveilleux entre nous. Parfois je m'oblige à l'aimer mais ça ne va pas au-delà de mes réserves de volonté' (p. 32) ('If I loved her, it would be really marvellous between us. Sometimes, I force myself to love her, but it is beyond my reserves of will power'). Having told him that she is pregnant, Karine makes clear to him that, as the *father*, he had to be the first to know. Mike writes that he feels really moved, to the point of having tears in his eyes. But he puts his sensitivity down to his fatigue and issues himself the following warning: 'Reprends-toi, mon vieux Mike, tu perds tout à fait les pédales!' (p. 34) ('Watch it, Mike, you are really losing it!'). He can't afford to let emotions get the better of him, otherwise he is likely to lose his control. In this instance, I would contend that the word that unsettled him emotionally and crossed his defences is 'father'.

Winer displays a total inability to have any compassion either towards the Other or towards himself. He drives himself, does not take care of his flat or of his health, hardly paying any attention to nutrition as long as he has cigarettes and alcohol; all the signs of self-neglect are here. 'This difficult start in life has left a deep and indelible mark on me'; the one phrase he writes about the trauma of his family being wiped out rings true. As well as not loving Karine, he does not appear to love or to have loved anyone else. At one point, when they are both in hospital, he keeps in touch with Mona Hessler. This fact could point to his being closer to her than to Karine, but as soon as they both know that they are HIV-positive, there is no more contact between them, and he writes that he does not have any need to ring her (p. 190).

There is no more compassion, let alone love, for the child that Karine is carrying. When he finds out that she is pregnant, he seriously considers denying that he is the father, going so far as to do some research in the library, and to read up on the accuracy of paternity tests (p. 37). Later on, he does not soften up in any way, even when he can feel the baby moving or sees photographs of the fœtus. The fact that the baby could be carrying the HIV virus does not seem to worry him except on one occasion (p. 139). It is significant that when Karine broaches the idea of having a child, he panics, protesting, in his own words, that he wants to live first (p. 32).

I want to argue that Winer is still being detached and avoiding the pain and grief he fears will totally overwhelm him. It is possible that having a child and becoming the father of this child would reunite him with some of his pain and loss, and he is not emotionally ready to go through with this. After Karine has announced that she is pregnant, he reflects that the birth of a child will not pose a problem to her rich family, even if 'le père n'a pas un centime, qu'il meurt dans un accident de la circulation ou qu'il disparaît sans laisser d'adresse! Un père, pour ces gens-là, ça va ça vient!' (p. 35) ('the father is penniless, he dies in a road traffic accident, he disappears without a forwarding address! For these people, a father comes and goes!'). One can feel palpable anger in Mike. It is the only time he opens up slightly about what it must have been like for him as a 16-year-old to be penniless, to have lost his father, and to have had to fight to get grants in order to carry on with his formal education (p. 13). The implicit message here is that, for him, a father is not a disposable commodity, and that in fact he has not found another one (a parallel issue is the complete silence surrounding his sister and mother). There is also an immediate association between the prospect of *becoming* a father and his having *lost* his father, which seems to confirm my analysis about his fiancée's pregnancy opening up his pain and loss. His familiar way of dealing with pain and loss is to dissociate, or split in psychoanalytical terms.

We saw above that the two instances of Winer displaying emotion (first of all almost softening up with Karine and then getting angry) are linked to the word 'father', and this makes me want to probe further in this direction. Mike Winer is not seeking a partner, a wife or a child. This is perhaps why he displays such scant attention to them. Mike Winer is seeking the family he lost when he was the child, or more accurately – because of his developmental age at the time – seeking a father. Following the first Sunday spent with the Wooleys, he writes that they have adopted him (the choice of 'adopt' indicating that he considered himself an orphan); for the first time in ages he belongs to a family where individuals help each other, and it gives him a reassuring feeling that he is no longer alone fighting in the world (p. 53). When he becomes ill and Mr Wooley comes to see him in his flat, he writes that he suddenly feels that he is his authentic son (p. 111). If one thinks of his relationship to older men, he is looking for a father-figure and, at the same time, he wants to be respected by that father-figure as a separate entity, hence there is a constant friction between them. So there is a degree of dependency, and a certain resentment of this very feeling. This is perhaps the developmental stage of a 16-year-old, his age when the car crash happened. This reading seems evident in view of the various fatherly figures in Winer's life.

His relationship with his 'formidable' boss at work, known as 'K.L.', is a good example. Winer is one of the few to command the respect of the boss. Likewise he projects onto 'M.G. Wooley', his future father-in-law, the image of an omnipotent father. It is no coincidence that both of them are described as smoking large cigars. A Freudian reading would no doubt point to the symbolic phallus; powerful, rich men. This is why Winer is so bitterly disappointed when 'M.G.' tells him that he knows 'K.L.' and that it was he who convinced 'K.L' to put Mike in charge of the investigation. Winer obviously believed he had been given the job on merit by 'K.L.' rather than through nepotism (p. 52). On a fantasy level, he had temporarily been recognised by the omnipotent father. Both Inspector Weiss (who seems to feel sorry for him and starts to watch over him) and Dr Burr also appear to be seen as fatherly figures.

I have claimed that Winer wanted a family in which he would be positioned as a child, and especially that he wanted a father, rather than a wife and a child. But I have also pointed to his own ambivalence in this desire. This is clearly illustrated by an episode when Inspector Weiss visits him at home. Winer states that he is angry, even with himself, but he directs his anger out and onto Weiss. The latter tells him he has come to visit out of 'sympathy' (p. 145) but is soon made to leave; Winer suggests to him that his wife is likely to be sleeping around, with the long unsociable working hours he keeps, and that he is therefore a future PWA. When Weiss has gone, Winer starts to feel remorseful, dreams about it during the night, thinks about it when he is awake, and wonders whether it was necessary to 'destabilise Weiss, and refuse his friendship to feel better about himself' (p. 147) when in fact he is left with no 'self-esteem'. This is a very revealing remark. For his self-esteem is somehow bound up with his relationship to an imaginary father-figure, in this particular episode, Weiss. But at the time, he refused Weiss's 'sympathy' in order to hurt him. His anger is getting the better of his neediness.

If emotionally Winer is hankering for a father-figure, he is himself an adult, and he is also in competition with this father-figure. The best example of this is his interaction with Mr Wooley, likely to become his own *father*-in-law. As well as being at the head of a formidable empire, he is described by the narrator as someone who was a man at the age of 12 (this is not explained but presumably he started work at 12), and a war veteran at 22, a man who has come face to face with *terror* during the war. Winer himself is now 23, and he can't help but make a comparison: 'Quand on a un beau-père comme ça, on se sent tout petit garçon auprès de ce valeureux guerrier […]' (p. 36) ('When you have a father-in-law like that, you feel like a really little boy compared to this valorous warrior […]'). For Winer, the construction of masculinity means proving oneself by some kind of heroic action where one's life is put on the line, as in ancient rites of initiation. Interestingly enough, he describes his investigation in the following terms: 'Depuis que j'ai commencé mon enquête, j'évolue dans le monde de la *terreur*. Qui disait qu'il faudrait une bonne guerre pour dresser notre génération […]' (p. 46) ('Since I have started my investigation, I navigate in the world of *terror*. Who said that our generation needed a proper war to teach us a lesson […]', my emphasis). Earlier he had used the word 'terror' to describe what Mr Wooley had encountered during the war. Hence, his investigation is his way of fighting his war, and coming face to face with terror is a necessary evil for him in order to deserve being called a man and no longer 'a really little boy'; it is something like a rite of passage. He must experience sheer terror too, because this is what sorts out men from boys. So his risk-taking and route to self-destruction may be more intentional than I had anticipated at first: being killed by the Mafia may be the equivalent for him of being killed by a stray bullet during a war. At another level, his high-risk sexual behaviour almost ensures that he will eventually become HIV-positive. His internalised construction of heterosexual desire combined with his grief response lead him to self-destruct; as Staudacher writes, unresolved or inhibited grief does not disappear as time passes, but rather it accumulates or finds destructive channels.[27]

I would like to end this chapter by going back to the car crash episode in view of Staudacher's remark about finding destructive channels. At a stroke Winer lost his father, his mother and his sister, at a time when he needed to establish his independence, aided by a powerful identification with his father. 'Tu es brusquement retiré du monde des vivants, de ceux qui peuvent toujours faire des projets pour leur boulot, la famille, les vacances et, cependant, tu es encore là' (p. 42) ('You are suddenly withdrawn from the living world, from those who can always elaborate plans for their work, their family, their holidays and yet, you are still there'). This description could be Winer describing what happened to him after the car crash, but in fact it is Bert Coffman describing what it is like to be diagnosed with AIDS. However, the parallel, and my argument, is that Winer could have *willed* this situation, because it is a familiar emotional place for him to be in. Metaphorically, he is revisiting the emotional scene of the car crash; his road to dying of bone cancer could have been sign-posted by himself. If he has built part of his subjectivity in this hollow place, then he has invested considerably in staying in that place. His whole emotional life calls for him to be in a situation where he will be face to face with death again. Alternatively, he could have been experiencing the well-known phenomenon of 'survivor's guilt' and be wanting to act on it; again, because so few details are given in the book, it is not possible to elucidate this further. Coffman's description occurs relatively early in the book. By the end of the book, it will totally fit Winer's situation. He will be alone in the world, just as he found himself alone when his family perished; no visits, no phone calls (p. 194).

There will be one last visitor, and it is paradoxically the one man he had mocked as being boring because he led too predictable a life: Philip (p. 197). Philip's relationship with Charlotte has continued to blossom and they now have a daughter. Winer reflects that Philip is certain not to get AIDS in view of his monogamy, concluding that it is surely Philip who was right. His own inability to love means he will have completely destroyed his 'adoptive' family. He has broken the heart of Mr and Mrs Wooley, and of their daughter. They all face a grim future, and are at that stage not sure that the child to be born is not also contaminated. When Mr Wooley leaves him for the last time, Winer writes that his own heart is broken and that he has a formidable feeling of guilt (p. 192), a great contrast to his earlier feeling when he described himself as Mr Wooley's authentic son. Symbolically, he has lost his father twice. He has put his adoptive family in the emotional place in which he found himself on two occasions in his own life: they too have gone from having everything to total destruction. His unresolved (gendered) grief, combining with his reading of masculine sexuality, has found the ultimate destructive channel, both for himself and for others.

During his stay in hospital, which corresponds to the final months of his life, all his energy is concentrated on writing his book. This process mirrors that of Juliette, who also starts writing her story from her hospital bed, as well as Simonin who starts to write when he is in the relative safety of the rest home; they are all retrospective narratives. It is almost after the point when people have fragmented (Winer talks for the first time about crying, pp. 180, 185) that they can start the painstaking process of rebuilding themselves. For there is no doubt that the painful and by its very nature reflexive process of writing his own story – even dressed up as a thriller – is a way for Mike Winer to start owning up to some of his feelings and to start bridging the gap caused by the splitting. Hence his urgent desire to be able to finish writing the story (p. 195): it is more than simply a story that is at stake. There is also some sort of reintegration of his feelings;[28] this sense of urgency is also found in Juliette and in Simonin. Writing appears to be a desperate, albeit indirect, manner of connecting his own life with that of other young people, so that they don't follow the same path as his. He states that this is his only ambition (p. 197). And his lesson to them is clear: 'For one minute of pleasure, I got myself a death sentence'

(p. 193). His imaginary audience is really the only one he hopes to connect with or shows any empathy with. This critical distance is related to a history of denial, starting with the grief episode. In the event, Winer's writing is interrupted by death. The book has a closure, but the closure seems to be the responsibility of another (Dr Burr, Winer's friends, the editor, or the real author behind the pseudonym Mike Winer, the inventor of a fictional narrative).

What is explicit in *Bienvenue dans le monde du Sida!* is that heterosexual monogamous sexuality is the only way to be and stay safe from the 'killer' virus. As Winer admits himself, it is surely Philip who was right in his outlook on life. So the model that is presented to us as the one where 'you don't catch AIDS' (p. 196) is Philip, his wife Charlotte (fulfilling her function of procreation) and their daughter. *Welcome to the World of Regulated Sexuality!* is a title that could have been given to this book, as equally to all the other AIDS fictions that we have studied.

Part II

AIDS Testimony

4 Testimony, Self-Avowal and Confession

This chapter brings together two instances of AIDS writing as testimonial. My reading will concentrate on the autobiographical nature of these texts but this approach is not meant to undermine the testimonial 'spirit' which was emerging in France as early as 1986. These testimonies were a political gesture intended to perform a particular political act through a particular statement, which then becomes more than personal. But this writing had to 'assert' itself against the AIDS fiction which, as I showed in Part I, mirrored the social attitudes of the time. This testimonial writing offers a contrast with the exploitative narratives of the fiction and with the kinds of views and attitudes represented by it. Testimonial authenticity is the opposite of exploitative narratives, with their conventional plots and stereotypes. As products of the popular culture industry, the latter are part of the problem that testimonial is up against. Simonin and Aron (and later Dreuilhe) are trying to express what it is like to live as an HIV-positive person. Testimonial writing is not only personally therapeutic but also an attempt to diagnose the social pathologies that are responsible for the embattlement of AIDS subjects, pathologies which are so embedded in society that they are not recognised as pathologies. Because of this context, testimonial writing runs a high risk of failing in its enterprise: speaking into the blind spots of society there is the danger of remaining invisible, unseen, unheard. This could explain why there is a fine line between testimony, self-avowal and confession. Simonin's book is constructed as self-avowal, and a narrative of guilty confession is superimposed on Aron.

Simonin: The Forgotten Witness

Neither in *L'Épidémie. Carnets d'un sociologue, Les Écrivains sacrifiés des années sida* nor *Le Rose et le noir*[1] is there any mention of Michel Simonin or of his book *Danger de vie*.[2] The book is out of print and its author is a forgotten witness. As the publisher has been taken over there is no possibility of consulting the press-cutting file, and I am told that there is no trace of this author in the old catalogues. Did Michel Simonin and his book really exist?[3] Not for Paillard, anyway: he writes that Dreuilhe was the first French-speaking author to have broken the silence on the subject of AIDS, whereas Dreuilhe's book was published a year after Simonin's.

As we saw in Chapter 1, *Danger de vie* was not the first account of AIDS to appear in France, but it represents an important intervention in AIDS testimony. It should be noted too that Simonin used other media to get himself heard. Where the written press was concerned, in addition to occasional contributions to *L'Événement du Jeudi* and *Gai Pied*, he wrote numerous letters to the editor of *Libération*, particularly in 1985 and 1986, some of which sparked off heated debates (pp. 58, 206).[4] Simonin was also an assiduous correspondent, writing to artists about AIDS (p. 300), as well as to Georgina Dufoix, the then Minister of Social Affairs and Solidarity (p. 70). As for television, he took part in four broadcasts between 1982 and 1986, testifying on one occasion anonymously and the other times openly, and also a programme for which it was decided at the last moment not to use his anonymous testimony.[5] I will be concentrating here mainly on his writing in *Danger de vie* and drawing upon Simonin's various statements on television to highlight my remarks, while bearing in mind that the two media both carry political significance.

Danger de vie is an autobiographical book. Published in 1986, it is above all a document on Simonin's life and on the 1980s that needs to be viewed in the context of the period. As we saw in the introduction, PWAs could not rely on a sense of solidarity nor on a community in France; they were mostly isolated. Simonin offers a striking contrast with the intellectual milieu in Paris or Belgium as it is represented in the artistic works of Hervé Guibert, Cyril Collard and Pascal de Duve.[6] He was a teacher before finding temporary jobs, often in the gay community. After that he was unemployed, and then, when his unemployment benefit ran out, he worked as a male prostitute in order to have a roof over his head. He ended up living on the street, sleeping in stairwells; he was also a drug addict.

The story of AIDS in the 1980s is one of attitudes of rejection and mechanisms of exclusion. Thus, when Simonin tells us about a stay in hospital in 1983, he recalls that the doctors and nurses were masked and gloved, that a red disc was stuck on his door and that his washing-up was done in his basin (p. 278). His experience of discrimination could be summed up in the following sentence: 'Pour moi, le virus qui me squatte est moins dangereux que l'isolement auquel on voudrait me condamner' (p. 240) ('For me, the virus squatting in me is less dangerous than the isolation they would like to condemn me to'). Simonin's various written accounts and his television appearances are of great importance when the circumstances of the time are recalled: the ACT-UP collective stresses that before 1987 only the newspaper *Gai Pied* and associations committed to fighting AIDS were involved in campaigns of information and prevention.[7] It is clear that most of the information available circulated in the media. Thus the career journalist Juliette in *Pourquoi moi?* describes getting research done for broadcasts and interviews on AIDS in order to gather information about her own diagnosis which had just been made. In all probability she would have seen the broadcasts in which Simonin appeared, at least those in 1985 and 1986.

Thus it can be seen that his contributions were far from unimportant: broadcast in the journalistic and political field, they functioned as

an act aimed at legitimating a political voice on AIDS that was independent of the medical authorities. This in turn introduced a distinction
between those who dared to speak out and those who kept silent, leaving
pronouncements to the experts. Simonin's intervention transgressed
the limits which until then had been respected by writers. When one
person steps out of line it calls into question the restrained attitude of
the others. That Simonin is no longer seen or heard in works on
literature and AIDS is one thing, but it should not be forgotten that,
in speaking out through television and the press, he cleared the way for
authors such as Dreuilhe.

What is *Danger de vie* like? Several genres are specified in the book.
Simonin speaks of a 'chronique' (p. 216) ('chronicle'), and subsequently
of 'confessions' (p. 247) ('confessions/avowals'). In the closing pages
the following can be read: 'J'arrive au terme de ces confidences impu-
diques. Autobiographie d'une vie chaotique, où je me révèle avec mes
contradictions, mes tourments, mes réflexions parfois acerbes ou banales'
(pp. 305–06) ('I am coming to the end of these shameless secrets. An
autobiography of a chaotic life, in which I reveal myself with my contradictions, my torments and my occasionally caustic or banal reflections').
The book's rhythm is sustained by the intertwining of the confessions
(which often correspond to a return to the past)[8] with the chronicle
(which often uses the present tense) and the confidences that bestraddle
the two modes. A preface by Dr Rozenbaum precedes the text, which
is made up of three parts. 'Un incident de parcours' (pp. 17–59) ('A
chance event') – in which the first date mentioned is June 1986 –
recounts Simonin's life in the first person from February 1985, the
date of his pre-AIDS diagnosis, onwards. Pre-AIDS or ARC (AIDS-
related complex) is today an obsolete term, but it was used in the
1980s. The catalogue of opportunistic infections to which he was
subject well and truly designates an HIV-positive person who would
have been clinically classified as having developed AIDS-related
illnesses. This narrative ends on Friday 13 September 1985, the date of
his arrival at the convalescent home of Praz-Coutant in Haute-Savoie.
His stay there, which was to last until 3 November 1985 (that is, a
little over seven weeks), takes up the greater part of the book (pp. 64–

292). Appropriately called 'Journal' ('Diary'), this narrative follows the day-by-day convention of the genre. Apart from details about Simonin's daily routine, we are offered a retrospective view, starting from his birth on 13 January 1952 (p. 74) and moving forward to July 1985. As a general rule these meditations on the past take place in the evening, and towards the end of the book Simonin tells the story to Christine, the night nurse who comes to listen to him. He often picks up the thread where he left off the previous evening, but he has to speed up when he notices that the day of his departure has arrived while he still has to cover the period from early 1983 to July 1985. The third part of the narrative is a brief 'Conclusion' and its setting is Simonin's return to Paris (pp. 295–306).

Hence the book is made up of two modes: descriptions of every-day life and a look back into the past. At the level of the former, things verge on banality: a typical day begins with waking up, with what the weather is like, with the treatments prescribed, and ends with long descriptions of the television programmes Simonin watches. He is himself conscious that his diary 'ressemble parfois à un hebdo de programme télé' (p. 303) ('sometimes resembles a weekly TV magazine'), but his comment is this:

> Pourra-t-on comprendre que dans une telle situation, aussi inconfortable, on se raccroche à peu de choses: à un écran de télévision qui constitue l'unique fenêtre ouverte sur le monde, parce qu'on veut à tout prix éviter la coupure totale, à des faits qu'on vit de loin et de près à la fois, et qui vous donnent la sensation d'exister encore? (p. 22)

> Will people be able to understand that in such an uncomfortable situation you cling to the little things: to a television screen which constitutes the only window opening on to the world because you want at all costs to avoid a complete break, and to events which you experience both from afar and close to, and which give you the feeling of still existing?

There is no hand-to-hand struggle with the virus as in Dreuilhe. The key word is 'exister' ('exist'): everything centres on Simonin's subjective impressions, feelings, experiences.

It seems appropriate at this stage to recall the view put forward by Murray Pratt in his book *Viral Discourse*,[9] in which he writes: 'Autobiographical discourse, seen from this perspective, becomes a cultural practice which benefits its speaker or author first and foremost, and listeners or readers only in so far as they approach the life story with a sense of esteem and respect [...] For many the recolonisation of a sense of self is the greatest victory possible.' So instead of judging Simonin's merits as a television critic I want to respect the inner struggle which these pages testify to. My reading of this text will concentrate on the author's subjectivity, following Hollway's understanding of the word: 'My approach to subjectivity is through the meanings and incorporated values which attach to a person's practices and provide the powers through which he or she can position him- or herself in relation to others.'[10]

The greater part of *Danger de vie* is taken up with the analysis of Simonin's past from his birth to the present time. There is a whole reading to be done here concerning the construction of his sexual discourse: this part of the text describes his world-weariness and his quest to position himself within a homosexual discourse, a possibility which only becomes realisable when he sees that he *wants* to position himself within this discourse. The cultural context within which Simonin operates betrays the difficulties of 'coming out' in France where there was a very different tradition of homosexualities from that of the United States or the United Kingdom. Following his first sexual encounter with a man, he writes, 'En sortant de chez lui, je n'étais pas encore certain de cette identité particulière: je ne la niais pas, mais je n'étais pas sûr, je ne savais pas' (p. 138) ('On leaving his place I was not yet certain of this particular identity: I was not in denial, but I was unsure, I did not know'). Living in Paris after that, his quest for a homosexual 'community' was confined to encounters in anonymous hotels and meetings at the houses of paedophiles; he comments that having wished to get close to this world he realised that it was not his own (p. 167). After his mother's death he was prepared to claim a homosexual 'identité'[11] ('identity') and began by writing about it to every member of his family. By 1981 he had got round to telling all his friends, explaining, 'Il fallait que je le dise, que je le crie! C'était l'essentiel de mon discours, je ne parlais que de cela, voulais qu'on me connaisse pour ce que j'étais' (p. 247) ('I had to say it, I had to shout it out loud! It was all I could talk about, I spoke of little else, I wanted people to know me for what I was'). It was at this time that he wrote offering to appear openly on the television show 'Aujourd'hui la vie', the topic being homosexuality. The programme was broadcast in the afternoon, and before it went out he again wrote to everyone in his family, particularly his father, to alert them to the fact; his letters were ignored (p. 250). The significant thing is that at a time when he had no opportunistic illness and when it can be assumed that he was not yet HIV-positive, Simonin the political activist appeared on television demanding to be accepted as a homosexual.

According to Diana Fuss's analysis, 'to be out is really to be inside the realm of the visible, the speakable, the culturally intelligible'.[12] How was it that he managed to appear on television? He was probably one of the few people to agree to testify openly, which again highlights the difficulties of 'role-models' in France; Simonin was a real pioneer. The burden of his discourse was the fact that he was a teacher and 'qu'on peut être à la fois éducateur et homosexuel et qu'on n'est pas pour autant des agresseurs, des violeurs, des monstres...' ('that one can be both a teacher and a homosexual and one is not for all that an aggressor, a rapist, a monster...'). Here he is trying to change a discourse of shame into a discourse of pride. Shortly afterwards he wrote, 'Je poursuivis ma folle existence avec le sentiment d'avoir mis un terme à une certaine forme de clandestinité, de vivre enfin, au grand jour, au sein d'une communauté solidaire, d'appartenir à une famille sociale organisée, de me sentir protégé' (p. 251) ('I pursued my crazy existence with the feeling of having put an end to a certain way of being clandestine, of living openly at last within a community showing solidarity, of belonging to an organised social family, of feeling safe and protected'). This feeling of belonging to a family was very important in view of the fact that everything was about to collapse.

I mentioned earlier Simonin's financial situation. The fact that he was unemployed, that he had no social status, was a very important element as far as his psychological state was concerned. He had no social 'identity': 'Au bout d'un an et demi de chômage indemnisé, succédant à de précédentes prises en charge des ASSEDIC, je me retrouve *sans statut précis* [...]' (p. 265, my italics) ('After a year and a half of unemployment benefit, following earlier payments by the unemployment insurance organisation, I found myself *without precise status* [...]'). The AIDS diagnosis made this crisis worse; as Zulian and Grandpierre point out in their work *Sida, Paroles intimes et nouvelles donnes*, 'Le sida pose la question de l'identité et de l'altérité [...] l'impact du virus sur nos modes de vie remet en cause le lien social, nos relations aux autres.' ('AIDS poses the question of identity and otherness [...] the impact of the virus on the way we live our lives casts doubt on the social bond, on our relations with others.')[13] One of the ways of reaffirming his subjectivity was his sexuality. Simonin was going to change his sexual habits completely and even end up not having sex at all, something which would in turn destabilise his newly found sense of 'identity'.

Another important element in Simonin's crisis of subjectivity is the fact that he laid claim, not only throughout his book but also in his last television appearance (16 December 1986), to the status of pre-AIDS. At a later point Simonin declared that he wished to 'en arriver au stade terminal de la maladie' (p. 20) ('reach the terminal stage of the disease'), being fed up with the pre-AIDS status which struck him as similar to that of a prisoner condemned to the electric chair waiting years on death row. The term then became para-AIDS, and all it meant for Simonin was the feeling that he was unclassifiable (p. 40). In fact this sense of unclassifiability, linked to the insecurity of his social status, shook his subjectivity, as he himself lucidly commented in the following sentence: 'Peut-être parce que je n'entrais dans aucune catégorie précise et que je n'avais pas de statut social, je voulais qu'on me considère, qu'on me reconnaisse, qu'on me classe [...]' (p. 40) ('Perhaps because I belonged to no precise category and had no social status, I wished to be considered, to be recognised, to be classified [...]'). So it can be seen that on all fronts Simonin had come to a true identity crisis.

What happened when Simonin was diagnosed as pre-AIDS? *Danger de vie* tells how Simonin's partner dropped him. In the cloakroom of the gay disco where he worked, this is what took place: 'Certains clients, me reconnaissant, ne voulaient pas me confier leurs vêtements, d'autres évitaient de me serrer la main… Et ce n'était pas de la parano de ma part, quelques-uns me l'ont confirmé: j'avais le SIDA et je faisais peur…' (p. 52) ('Some customers who recognised me would not let me take their clothes, others avoided shaking my hand… And this was not paranoia on my part: some confirmed to me that I put the wind up people because I had AIDS…'). He then changed jobs, but the owners of the bar which took him on sacked him too in due course. This is a far cry from Simonin saying, once he came out as a homosexual, that he belonged to a community showing solidarity, an 'organised social family' (p. 251). Because he is pre-AIDS, he meets with rejection and discrimination. It illustrates the fact that gay men in France felt totally isolated, and that there was no solidarity for PWAs; the ghetto was full of paranoia, as Woods's analysis points out (see introduction).

After he had left Paris and the discrimination he suffered within the gay community in order to get his strength back, Simonin's stay at Praz-Coutant became another tale of discrimination. We are here merely at one remove from the 'pesthouses' for PWAs advocated at the time by Jean-Marie Le Pen. The convalescent home was prepared to accept pre-AIDS patients 'pour respecter le taux de fréquentation du centre, dont dépend la fixation des prix de journées' (p. 240) ('in order to conform to the rate of take-up in the centre on which the per-diem charge depends'), but on certain conditions. Simonin had to be in a single room and take all his meals there. They even got him a television set so that he did not have to use the common rooms. They gave him a bottle of bleach to use each time he went to the toilet (p. 71), and the doctor advised him to lie if the others asked him why he did not eat with them. Simonin was treated like a leper, forced to deny his condition, in an echo of the label of 'gay plague'. According to Lévy and Nouss's analysis,

> Le contrôle social qui s'exerce sur les malades a pour objectif et pour effet de les isoler, faisant passer la définition de la maladie du pathologique au

déviant. En ce sens, le sida, maladie moderne, rejoignait le cortège des maladies épidémiques qui, au cours de l'histoire, ont stigmatisé les sujets atteints.[14]

The social control exercised on patients has the aim and effect of isolating them, causing the definition of the disease to slide from the pathological to the deviant. In this sense, AIDS, a modern illness, was joining the cortège of epidemic diseases which have throughout history stigmatised those suffering from them.

Simonin's carefully constructed subjectivity was now dismantled: the homosexual milieu rejected him, he suffered a complete loss of libido, and his status as a pre-AIDS person meant that he was treated like a pariah.

I mentioned earlier that in one of the television broadcasts it was decided at the last minute not to use his testimony. The symbolic dimension of this episode is significant: Simonin was no longer free to speak and found himself without a voice. As soon as he arrived at Praz-Coutant he informed the doctor that a television crew was to come and interview him about AIDS. Faced with the discriminatory measures to which he had been subjected, he did not mind letting it be known that he was going to denounce them (p. 65). A few days later he was informed that the management were categorically opposed to the interview taking place (p. 91), not because of the tenor of any remarks he was likely to make, but because they did not wish it to be known that PWAs were admitted to their institution, since this might result in a reduction in the overall intake of residents. A compromise was reached: he was allowed to appear before the cameras outside the centre's precincts, on neutral territory, in Switzerland no less, at Geneva airport. It needs to be stressed that Simonin risked a great deal by not giving in: the management were thinking of expelling him at once (p. 98). He had neither income, nor social security, nor housing in Paris, so would have found himself back on the streets. He was none-theless prepared to risk all that in order to speak out, even when told repeatedly that someone on high was said to have declared 'qu'il était inadmissible qu'un malade prenne la parole et qu'on ne devrait pas parler du SIDA, parce que c'est une maladie mortelle!' (p. 98) ('that it was unacceptable for a patient to speak to the media, and that AIDS should not be talked about, because it was a deadly illness!').

Simonin decided to testify anonymously so as not to prejudice his chances of getting another job in Paris (p. 103). A fortnight or so after the filming had taken place he read in *Libération* the television critic's preview of the evening's programme (p. 158) and heard in an extract from the programme broadcast on the television news at lunchtime the testimony of a patient openly declaring, '[…] il n'y a pas de maladie honteuse, seulement des malades honteux' ('[…] there are no shameful illnesses, only ashamed ill people'). Simonin thought at once that this declaration labelled him as ashamed because he wished to remain anonymous. But he did not appear on television. Having found another PWA who agreed to appear in person – a scoop for the channel (p. 159) – Simonin was sacrificed. They did not even have the decency to let him know.[15] What mattered to the programmers was the witness's *face*; too bad if he had nothing much to say or if Simonin would have had more interesting things to talk about. We never find out the identity of this PWA, but from his conversation we can deduce that he is well-off, and he states that he is a university professor.

Simonin was not jealous of the witness, but he did remark that, given the latter's social situation, he was not taking too many risks in appearing on television whereas he, Simonin, had wished to remain anonymous in the hope of getting another job. He did not want the viewers to imagine that 'les victimes du SIDA vivent tous,[16] sinon dans des conditions privilégiées, du moins à l'abri des soucis matériels' (p. 159) ('AIDS victims all live, if not in privileged circumstances, at least shielded from material worries').

Pollack's analysis of this episode is as follows: 'Contestant donc à ce professeur la qualité de témoin d'une cause commune, R. [Simonin] s'attribue indirectement ce privilège à cause de la similitude entre la situation des malades les plus démunis et la sienne' ('So, questioning this professor's capacity as witness in a common cause, R. indirectly attributes this privilege to himself because of the similarity between the situation of the most deprived patients and his own').[17] Pollack's analysis goes on to stress that Simonin constructs for himself an 'identity' as patient in which he enhances the value of the disease experience as a specific qualification.[18] Has he not the right to legitimate this approach? When one sees on 'Le Magazine' the professor in his opulent apartment saying that his sole preoccupation is 'Should I go on building my library and buying books?', one is worlds away from Simonin who was about to find himself back on the streets without social security cover; Simonin's action has nothing to do with shame. Why should he not enhance the value of his experience as a PWA in terms of a specific qualification? How can he be seen and heard in a culture that wishes to make him invisible and silent, a culture in which 'les caractéristiques principales de l'expérience de la maladie sont le secret et le silence' ('the chief characteristics of the experience of the disease are secrecy and silence')?[19]

Let us rather see his reaction: 'Je ressens un besoin viscéral d'écrire et envoie une longue lettre sur ce qui se passe ici au courrier des lecteurs de *Libération*' (p. 160) ('I feel a visceral need to write and send a long letter about what is happening here to the editor of *Libération*'). Simonin had a long history of engaging in correspondence to which he never received a reply; the first time he wrote to his family to speak about his sexual orientation no one answered (p. 213), any more than they did the second time (p. 250). Some of his letters to *Gai Pied* or to *Libération* were ignored. But on this occasion he was confounded: not only did *Libération* publish his letter, they put Praz-Coutant in the subhead. As Simonin says, he was going to have to take the consequences (p. 206). As we have seen, the board of governors contemplated expelling him (p. 209), but since he was due to leave a few days later, they decided to wait. Simonin's self-positioning within a discourse of political activism was perhaps his only mechanism of survival, helping him not to give in. This is Simonin's own analysis concerning the letters he sent to *Libération* from 1985 onwards: 'C'est peut-être grâce à l'envoi de ces lettres, grâce à cette possibilité de pousser publiquement un cri que j'ai trouvé en moi la force de réagir' (p. 42) ('It is perhaps thanks to the sending of those letters, thanks to the opportunity they gave me of making a public outcry, that I found in myself the strength to react').

We saw that after Simonin had decided to come out as a homosexual, he was rejected because he was HIV-positive, the rejection coming both from society at large and from the homosexual milieu. But *Danger de vie* is also the story of Simonin's struggle to emerge from this crisis; this is the most important and original aspect of his book.

In a work entitled *Le Traumatisme de la mort annoncée (Psychosomatique et Sida)*, Annette Thomé-Renault mentions certain types of psychological problems in HIV-positive people. The one that seems most closely to correspond to Simonin's case is the state of interruption of the preconscious link such that 'il existe une coupure entre le moi psychique et le ça corporel' ('there is a split between the psychological ego and the corporal id').[20] Basing her findings on interviews, Thomé-Renault stresses that following the failure of the preconscious, the subject proceeds to an 'énumération neutre des inconvénients de sa situation, ou il fait un récit dépourvu d'émotion des événements banals qui constituent la réalité actuelle quotidienne, énumérant parfois le déroulement chronologique des faits, précisant les horaires et les quantités [...]' ('neutral enumeration of the disadvantages of their situation, or they give an account lacking in emotion of the commonplace occurrences making up everyday reality, sometimes listing the chronological unfolding of events, specifying schedules and quantities [...]').[21] This reads like a description of *Danger de vie*, for what strikes one in Simonin's book is that, on first reading, it very often seems lacking in emotion(s), indeed in reflections on AIDS.

Thomé-Renault goes on to say that this type of asymptomatic depression frequently goes unnoticed and if it continues it can give rise to a long-lasting reign of the death instinct. As it happens, even if the diagnosis was not made until February 1985, Simonin knew that he was ill and probably HIV-positive from early 1983 onwards (pp. 277–78). During this period he was to make several attempts at suicide (pp. 57, 282, 285–86). According to Thomé-Renault again, when confronted with the depression following a failure of the preconscious, patients can get out of it if they undergo therapy in a treatment centre enabling a beneficial regression to take place, leading to a mental reconstruction.[22] This pattern corresponds to Simonin's real-life experience: coming from a situation in Paris where he had nowhere to live and his only meal of the day consisted of take-away sandwiches given him by the Salpêtrière staff (p. 56), he found himself in a convalescent home where he enjoyed about seven weeks of material security. Despite the extreme forms of discrimination he endured there he was able to devote himself to a period of reflection that was to prove beneficial.

The main component of the section headed 'Journal' ('Diary') in *Danger de vie* is the look back into the past. As it happens, this is a feature frequently encountered in books on AIDS. No longer having a future, or only an uncertain one, writers either (re)turn to their past, or else they feel the need to go back to a period before they were diagnosed as HIV-positive. That is the case with Simonin, who foresaw that his existence in Paris would be very precarious: 'Des angoisses m'assaillent, fondamentales, sur mon devenir, les conditions de ce que va être ma vie à Paris, sur ma solitude, sur mon abstinence aussi… Et je plonge dans mes souvenirs' (p. 162) ('I am assailed by deep feelings of anguish about my future, about the conditions of what is going to be my life in Paris, about my solitude, about my abstinence too… And I plunge back into my memories'). But that alone does not explain the look back into the past in *Danger de vie*.

Simonin describes his past life as being 'une fuite en avant' (p. 247) ('a flight forward'). This image of a flight is symbolic of someone who denies his suffering and is afraid of fragmentation. When the pre-AIDS diagnosis is announced, how can he experience his emotions when he has denied them for so long? Before our eyes, through the act of writing, a long therapeutic (re)apprenticeship takes place. That is what Simonin admits indirectly when he writes, 'J'ai tenu mon journal […] démarche ardue, parce qu'il est plus facile d'occulter un passé douloureux que d'aller à la recherche de soi-même' (p. 21) ('I have kept my diary […] a difficult thing to do, because it is easier to hide a painful past from view than to go in search of oneself'). The fragmentation in itself can have positive aspects since it makes possible the reconstruction of a sense of self: 'Je suis capable, aujourd'hui, d'affronter le passé, d'en parler sans douleur, d'avouer ce terrible mal de vivre qui m'a rongé pendant de longues années' (p. 296) ('I am capable, today, of confronting the past, of speaking about it without pain, of confessing this terrible uneasy feeling about living that has been gnawing away at me for many a long year').

This return to the past is painful: 'Cette descente dans mon passé ne me fait pas vraiment de bien. De retour à la réalité, je dois prendre des tranquillisants pour mettre fin à cet épouvantable tourment qui me bouffe, me prend aux tripes' (p. 139) ('This plunge into my past does not really do me any good. When I return to reality I have to take tranquillisers to put a stop to this dreadful torment which gnaws into me and socks me in the guts'). The regression consists in rediscovering deep within himself the pain that inhabits him, the permanent feeling of guilt for not having lifted his mother from her mediocre existence (p. 211). Little by little he regains possession of his pain: 'Qu'avec la disparition de ma mère, j'avais perdu le seul être que j'aimais et que rien ni personne ne pourrait remplacer' (p. 212) ('The fact that with my mother's death I had lost the only person I ever loved, whom nothing and no one could replace'). He also reintegrates his past sufferings, buried, denied, repudiated, quoting Fritz Zorn: 'Car c'est cela ma tâche: me délivrer du tourment écrasant de mon passé' (p. 297) ('For that is the task before me: to free myself of the crushing torment of my past'). This regression follows the period of 'flight forward' and precedes a 'nouvelle naissance' (p. 22) ('new birth').

Such is the sense in which, in my view, we should interpret this theme which runs through the book (for example, 'renaître', p. 43, 'to be reborn'), and which is the subject of one of the two retranscribed poems. There the process of flight/regression /rebirth is not yet explicit, but it is sensed through the tone of this poem which corresponds to a 'furieuse envie d'écrire' (pp. 141–42) ('furious longing to write'). The poem is addressed to a 'tu' (the familiar 'you') who has not yet been born (second line) but who will be what he ought to be once he is born (last sentence). The reparation (the look backwards) reconstitutes a sense of self that was fragmented. In the third part of the volume, set in Paris, the book's dénouement reflects this idea of a new birth ('C'est d'une nouvelle naissance, pour moi, qu'il s'agit' (p. 305) ('It's all about a new birth for me')), backed by a second quotation from Fritz Zorn:

'maintenant j'aurais enfin une chance de renaître à une vie nouvelle qui, peut-être, ne serait plus aussi cruelle que ma vie passée...' (p. 306) ('now I would at last have a chance to be reborn to a new life which, perhaps, would not be as cruel as my past life...'). This 'renaissance' ('rebirth') has a dual purpose, also making it possible for Simonin to confront his pre-AIDS status since, having embraced his painful past, he is ready to square up to his present situation.

In the midst of the disappearance of his sense of self, a possibility of restructuring thus appears, albeit at the metaphorical level. I should like to introduce here the metaphor of avalanche. This metaphor serves both to express what Simonin felt when the pre-AIDS diagnosis was confirmed, and – thanks to an anecdote which acts as a catalyst in the book – to legitimate his feeling of grief. He is able to feel legitimated, which in turn makes it possible for him to explore his feelings in the face of death.[23] In the absence of a French community that would hold him and allow him to grieve, Simonin – rather resourcefully – invents his own socially acceptable community.

In his book *The Psychology of Shame*, Gershen Kaufman writes, 'AIDS activates a sense of acute powerlessness and uncertainty. Whether actually receiving the diagnosis itself or only imagining oneself contracting the dreaded disease, the consequence is real or imagined *catastrophe*' (my emphasis).[24] The catastrophe imagined by Simonin, his visualisation of the virus, is the image of an avalanche. As early as the first part of the book, he describes in these terms the virus which he carries inside him and by virtue of which he has in his possession 'un pouvoir de mort [...] Il m'arrive de me considérer comme un volcan bouillonnant de lave mortelle!' (p. 19) ('a power of death [...] I sometimes think of myself as a volcano seething with deathly lava!'). During his mountain walks Simonin often stops in a clearing; later in the book, he learns that this spot to which he is unconsciously drawn and where he sunbathes was the scene of a catastrophe. On 17 April 1970 a mudslide engulfed a sanatorium, causing 79 deaths (p. 105). Four days after reading about the catastrophe he returns to the spot. The clearing is described as a 'cicatrice' (p. 112) ('scar'). He meditates as follows:

Je pense à cette calamité, imaginant la vie qui régnait ici quelques secondes avant le drame, puis à l'épouvantable chaos qui s'ensuivit; j'essaye de comprendre ce qui a pu se passer, avec une furieuse envie d'en savoir plus. J'entends dévaler la puissante coulée de boue [...] je la vois s'abattre violemment sur les bâtiments, dans un formidable vacarme. Un très court silence, terrible, puis les premiers gémissements, l'horreur... Les victimes sont essentiellement des enfants. (p. 113)

I think of this calamity, imagining life here a few seconds before the tragedy, then the frightful chaos that ensued; I try to understand what happened, with a furious urge to know more. I can hear the powerful mudslide rushing down [...] I see it crashing violently into the buildings in a colossal din. A very short silence, terrible, then the first groans, the horror... The victims were mainly children.

What we have here is a verbalisation by Simonin of the ravages caused in February 1985 by the news that he had pre-AIDS. I will clarify this. According to Lévy and Nouss,

Le Sida est un phénomène qui se définit autant au niveau de sa patho-logie que de sa sociologie, réception et perception. Or la métaphore est une figure de rhétorique et de pensée qui ne peut s'énoncer en dehors de sa dimension socio-discursive. La métaphore fonctionne à l'intérieur d'un cadre de signification global, d'un système historique et idéologique. Elle est investie sémantiquement si le code l'accueillant est connu et reconnaissable.[25]

AIDS is a phenomenon which is defined as much at the level of its sociology, reception and perception as of its pathology. Now, metaphor is a figure of rhetoric and of thought which cannot be expressed outside its socio-discursive dimension. The metaphor functions within a total frame-work of meaning, a historical and ideological system. It is semantically invested if the receiving code is known and recognisable.

A natural catastrophe in which *innocent children* are killed is a national tragedy in which everyone feels concerned and experiences a certain sympathy. The whole community usually rallies round such events and shows great solidarity. This avalanche had the function of legitimising

Simonin's grief. In that metaphorical space he had room to give free rein to his grief but also to explore death.

Simonin's social 'identity' was non-existent, he was pre-AIDS, he was subjected to discrimination, he did not appear on television; however, there still remained for him the metaphor of the avalanche by which, taking on temporarily the 'identity' of one of those innocent children swept away by the mud, he had a legitimate place in society's compassion. This is in contrast to the sort of remark he overheard relating to his condition, in which 'well-deserved punishment' for a 'depraved lifestyle' were the catch phrases (p. 110) – the familiar 'just punishment' narrative. From the moment he knew about the catastrophe he declared himself fascinated and wanting to know more, but without being aware of his motives (p. 113). The mere sight of photos of the centre before its destruction gave rise to a feeling within him resembling sadness, and he declared himself deeply troubled (p. 115). There is no doubt whatever that this sadness and this distress were his own: metaphorically, it was his seronegative body that he was looking at. He decided to gather eyewitness accounts, but soon came up against a wall of silence: litigation was in progress and no one was willing to talk. He had to abandon his project, commenting 'J'étais si heureux de m'être trouvé un but que je suis un peu déçu' (p. 115) ('I was so pleased to have found an aim that I am rather disappointed'). Simonin was able to stage in what he calls the 'tragédie' ('tragedy') (which therefore evokes the *pity* of others) the trauma of his physical deterioration, fear of death and utter powerlessness in the face of the diagnosis that had been made. By projecting himself into a form of collective grief he probably had the illusion of recovering a feeling of being in control, and he probably recovered (or discovered) a sense of community. (But it should be noted that this identification was double-edged: by engaging in it he perpetuated the image of HIV-positive people as victims, and thus legitimised another of the ways they were being depicted at the time.)

An exercise in historical periodisation would show that AIDS writing in France and elsewhere has gone through several phases. Before aspiring to the success of Christophe Bourdin's book *Le Fil*,[26] extracts from which were read on the radio on the occasion of World AIDS Day (1 December 1996) more or less everywhere in France and in French-speaking countries, AIDS writing at the outset had to be carefully coded. Simonin was one of the first to have tried to find an audience prepared to listen. This audience was not constituted overnight. Through his struggle to speak and testify in different media he demonstrates what happens when one is faced with a wall of silence, a phenomenon well understood by ACT-UP in its adoption of the slogan 'Silence = Mort' ('Silence = Death'). *Danger de vie* is important by virtue of its flaws (what the book does not manage to express about living with AIDS), but also by virtue of the symbolic significance of its author's being censored on television, and, even if its thrust is not far removed from that of a work such as *Le Protocole compassionnel* by Hervé Guibert,[27] because of its dedication to the idea of final redemption. It serves also as a useful reminder of the reality of life in France as a PWA in the early 1980s, where there was no gay community to speak of to support PWAs. The writing process in *Danger de vie* enabled Simonin to find new possibilities for living in the midst of death and to reinvent himself by means of his open testimony, an approach emphasised by the book's cover which features the author's photograph.[28]

It is all the more the pity that *Danger de vie* lends itself to recuperation in terms of the discourses about AIDS that dominated at the time, in a way that is fairly obvious and predictable: promiscuous homosexual men are likely to catch AIDS. By implication, staying 'safe' means being a monogamous heterosexual. The back cover text makes for interesting reading. After depicting Simonin as a completely depraved character, the tone of the last two paragraphs blossoms into optimism. Simonin is fighting with an 'hygiène de vie rigoureuse' ('rigorous healthy lifestyle'). This expression is deliberately ambiguous, because it could mean total sexual abstinence as well as a sensible diet and an exercise regime. The doctors are surprised: is there a possibility of remission from AIDS? This is followed by, 'Voici un livre d'aujourd'hui, écrit par un homme qui s'est découvert dans l'épreuve.' ('Here is a book for today, written by a man who found himself in an ordeal.') The message implied by the text is that, first of all, if you abstain from sexual relationships, you could have a *remission* from AIDS. Secondly, it is not in coming out as a homosexual but in abstaining from sex and in suffering that Simonin found his sense of self. This echoes Pascalian notions of Jansenism. Once more, as in the case of AIDS fiction, the back cover of *Danger de vie* could be constructed as an attempt at repression. Perhaps the book found a publisher because the story lends itself to recuperation of this kind or because the publishers knew they could play safe by means of the moralising blurb. Either way, it makes for a depressing analysis: this first instance of AIDS testimony does not seem totally to evade the 'just punishment' narrative evident in early AIDS fiction. As for the 'remission' suggested on the back cover blurb, within a year of the book's publication Simonin had died of AIDS-related illnesses.

Aron: The Overlooked Witness

'[In 1987] there occurred what many in France now view as a critical juncture in the history of the epidemic there: the publication of philosopher Jean-Paul Aron's article "Mon Sida" [...] Aron became the first French *personnalité* to speak openly to the media about his illness.'[29] Many people view Jean-Paul Aron's interview in *Le Nouvel Observateur* on 30 October 1987 as a watershed.[30] Aron, probably best known for his book *Les Modernes*,[31] chose an interview in a weekly magazine to discuss his illness, the interviewer being Elizabeth Schemla. The text of the interview was later reprinted as a monograph, *Mon sida*.[32] The title 'Mon sida' ('My AIDS') is an explicit statement by Aron that he has AIDS. He is also coming out as being a homosexual (which he does in the interview), and claiming AIDS as something that belongs to him. In the history of writing AIDS up to then, the word itself had often been omitted, or replaced by other words or metaphors.[33]

It is difficult to understand Harvey's point when he writes that although Aron writes 'mon sida', he *paradoxically* qualifies AIDS as "unnameable"' (my emphasis).[34] This remark denigrates Aron's political gesture as is clear when the exact context of his remark is considered:

J'ajoute que mes réactions vis-à-vis du *sida* jusqu'à ces dernières semaines, et ma gêne à me reconnaître tel que je suis, prouvent que j'ai été moi-même victime du cliché, du fantasme collectif face à une maladie innommable. Innommable, voilà le mot clé. (my emphasis) (p. 28)

An additional comment is that my reaction towards *AIDS* up to the last few weeks, and my embarrassed reluctance to recognise myself as I am, prove that I myself was a victim of the cliché, of the collective fantasy in the presence of an unnameable illness. Unnameable, that is the key word.

First of all, Aron does write *AIDS*; secondly, he only uses 'unnameable' to criticise his own attitude up to the point when he decided to go public. Aron is saying that *up until then* he colluded with the discourse of AIDS as unnameable, but this clearly is no longer the case. His interview is a personal re-claiming of his own subjectivity in the face of the dominant culture's making his illness 'unnameable' or culturally invisible. This is an act of courage since he risks being demonised or misunderstood.

Right at the very end of the interview, Aron states 'tous ces aveux me procurent un immense soulagement' (p. 31) ('all these confessions give me an immense sense of relief'). I have translated 'aveu' as confession, but it also translates as admission or avowal; confession carries with it a sense of guilt and repentance while admission or avowal are more neutral terms. I guess Aron chose to use 'aveu' being aware of the word's ambivalence. Unfortunately for him and independently of his will, people eager to perpetuate the 'just punishment' narrative tended to read 'aveu' as confession, rewriting his interview as a confessional act. We saw that this is quite typical of the reception of early AIDS writing, following a pattern Foucault describes in *The History of Sexuality*,[35] where the confessional mode is the form that power often takes. The interviewer, and by extension the readers, become the authority figures, with the power to absolve the repentant sinner. Confession is perhaps one of the few discursive modes which the dominant discourse is willing to allow in talking about HIV/AIDS. Simonin himself tentatively gives the label of confession to his book (p. 247);

this echoes the back cover of *Danger de vie* where we saw Simonin's story recuperated and (re)constructed.

Reactions to Aron's interview centred then around criticisms of what he said about guilt in relation to homosexuality:[36] 'Ma vérité, c'est que je suis un faisceau de culpabilités dans lequel l'homosexualité pèse lourdement mais pas uniquement' (p. 24) ('My truth is that I am an array of guilty feelings in which homosexuality weighs heavily but not exclusively'). The *coup de grâce* was 'Personne ne peut prétendre vivre la marginalité dans le bonheur' (p. 31) ('Nobody can pretend that living marginally brings on a state of happiness'). An 'array of guilty feelings' is a telling statement which contextualises the problematics of Aron's homosexuality within the Catholic tradition in France. This is beyond the scope of this book; however, among other factors, the Church's official line on homosexuality would be worth studying in depth in order to gain an understanding of what Aron is saying. But I want to try to prescind from the reception of the text and read it from my own subject-position in order to bring out a newer perspective, before returning to the issue of guilt.

We can begin by looking at the short text written by Schemla that precedes the interview which 'sets the scene'. It is the equivalent of the back cover blurb of the books we looked at earlier. It starts with a physical description of Aron as 'amaigri' ('thinner'), having a 'toux sèche' ('dry cough'), 'baillant de fatigue' ('yawning from tiredness'); it then risks extending the metaphor to his words which are described as 'dépouillés' (p. 7) ('stripped down'). Schemla is stereotyping Aron in terms of the cliché portrait of the PWA. She describes the AZT on the coffee table and the alarm clock which reminds him when to take the drug. Finally the first question is launched, why has he wanted to give this interview?

Diagnosed in January 1986, Aron describes having had various opportunistic illnesses, until he contracted PCP (Pneumocystis Carinii Pneumonia) on 26 July 1987 (p. 8). He was admitted to intensive care in hospital and had a brush with death. After coming out of hospital, he decided that he would talk openly about having AIDS and he describes this act as a partial liberation of himself (p. 9).

I see 'Mon sida' as a political project. It is a continuation of Jean-Paul Aron's sociological work, which has always operated at the margins of culture, and notably his ground-breaking book *Le Pénis et la démoralisation de l'Occident* (*The Penis and the Demoralization of the West*).[37] This is very much Aron's own reading too; he describes a process of liberation that he started with the aforementioned book and which is continuing with the present interview (p. 16). He shows great sensitivity to people like Simonin when he writes that being HIV-positive must be difficult when one is alone, poor and unknown (though instead of using the word positively, he uses 'malédiction', p. 30 ('curse')). He states quite clearly that he does not understand people who have almost nothing to fear and yet still remain(ed) silent. Famously, he criticises Michel Foucault for not having spoken about being HIV-positive, and he believes firmly that his was a silence of shame rather than that of an intellectual (p. 26). His next point is that he has attacked Foucault in the past (in *Les Modernes*) because he was jealous of the latter's fame (pp. 26–27). This shows that there are no double standards here, and that Aron is also being self-critical.

The political project of 'Mon sida' is also apparent in the socio-cultural comments included in the text. Aron is astounded by the peculiarity that AIDS was 'monitored' only by the press in the early 1980s; people were reading the press in order to access information since no government information campaigns existed (p. 11). The media became the only source of knowledge. Aron has no time for doctors who suddenly regained their symbolic power and their aura of respectability; he has even less time for the media who, according to him, acted irresponsibly by stigmatising homosexuals and talking about 'les victimes homosexuelles' (p. 12) ('homosexual victims'). Aron sharpens his analysis by stating that this was a way of taking back the new-found tolerance towards homosexuals (p. 13), and that no matter how many other groups were shown to be affected by the virus, it still remains in the West a homosexual 'disease'. This remark shows that homosexuals felt that the government's attitude to the AIDS crisis was a backlash against recent sexual liberation, and that the concessions obtained in the early 1980s were to be short-lived. Consequently, it

111

became once more very difficult to 'come out' as a homosexual in France, as one was almost immediately stigmatised as a potential 'killer' (an AIDS carrier, as some of the press put it). In passing, Aron criticises the French government's inaction, naming Michèle Barzach, as well as Le Pen's use of the crisis (pp. 28–29), and the state of neurosis over contamination (p. 29). Finally the over-reporting in the media is seen as overcompensation for the failure of science to halt the pandemic. Aron also clearly states that having AIDS is not a punishment (p. 22), countering the 'just punishment' narrative. In short, Aron sketches what gay activists would later flesh out.[38]

Aron was given his diagnosis over the phone by his brother who was a doctor (p. 17). He thinks he was infected by an American he met in Florence in December 1981 (p. 22), thus perpetuating the tradition in French texts of reading the virus as invading France from America. He describes receiving the diagnosis as a 'cataclysme' (p. 17) ('cataclysm'). This is comparable with Simonin's reactions on being diagnosed, and his subsequent use of the avalanche metaphor. Aron's reaction confirms Kaufman's analysis of shame (see above) and is very similar to that found in other PWAs' accounts, notably those of Hervé Guibert. At first, he used to weigh himself daily, and he was on red alert for any itching (p. 18); now he has even stopped weighing himself (p. 20). He has also decided not to lead an active sex life any more (p. 21). All is not as it seems though as Aron drops into the conversation that he is presently suffering from anorexia. This is not dwelt on, but it certainly indicates a psychic rebellion at some level.

The main phenomenon to be observed, one about which Aron is very lucid, is that after he learnt that he was HIV-positive, he started to become really dependent on his doctor brother, and began to regress totally. This response is found in many PWAs as recorded by Lévy and Nouss who talk about 'la régression psychologique individuelle provoquée par le sida (nostalgie de l'enfance et du passé) [...]' ('the individual psychological regression caused by AIDS (nostalgia for one's childhood and for the past)').[39] Having transcended this state, Aron is a little harsh with himself, talking about immaturity and masochism (p. 19). His new-found serenity, which allows him to speak about 'his AIDS', was preceded by a stay alone in the mountains, not unlike Simonin's stay in Praz-Coutant.

It is now time to revisit the reception of 'Mon sida' and specifically the question of guilt. I would start by quoting the feminist post-structuralist position about individual and social change:

> Consciousness-changing is not accomplished by new discourses replacing old ones. It is accomplished as a result of the contradictions in our positionings, desires and practices – and thus in our subjectivities – which result from the coexistence of the old and the new. Every relation and every practice to some extent articulates such contradictions and therefore is a site of potential change as much as it is a site of reproduction.[40]

In light of this position and bearing in mind Edelman's warning quoted in the introduction ('In the case of AIDS, infection endlessly breeds sentences'),[41] I believe that Aron's intentions were to bring about personal and social change, so that AIDS would no longer remain unnameable. It is also the case that some of his remarks (such as when he associates being HIV-positive with a 'curse') lend themselves to being perceived as reproducing conventional attitudes to the disease.

Aron has always operated from the margins, in the intellectual field, and also in terms of the homosexual milieu: '[…] je ne me suis jamais senti homosexuel' (p. 28) ('[…] I have never felt that I was a homosexual'). He believes that homosexuality is a form of marginality that society merely tolerates rather than readily welcomes (p. 30), and this would certainly have been the experience of homosexuals of his generation living in France. It appears that Aron was very much in the closet until 1982 when he started taking part in gay rights marches (p. 15). One cannot talk of 'coming out' as such, but it was the case that more homosexuals decided to have a certain degree of visibility, encouraged by the apparent liberalism brought about by the socialist government that had been in power since 1981 (for instance, Foucault started to give interviews in *Gai Pied*). Aron associates himself with Dandyism when explaining why he decided to hold the interview and defines this school of thought as absolute difference and singularity (p. 9). He has also spent all his life in the shadow of his older brother, the famous surgeon, and of his cousin Raymond Aron, the well-known intellectual. I don't want to suggest by this that Aron is a passive agent in any way. I think he *actively* chose the margins, perhaps because he thought it was the best way for him to be heard. The dandy who had constructed his whole positioning on absolute difference and singularity (one presumes with respect to the dominant discourse as embodied by his cousin Raymond Aron, though it is not made explicit) decided to declare both 'his AIDS' and his homosexuality, relegating this time not only Michel Foucault but all the other intellectuals who, according to him, had nothing to lose and yet chose to remain silent, to the margins of this present essay. He states: 'La maladie seule m'oblige à convenir que j'appartiens existentiellement et socialement à cette catégorie (des homosexuels)' (p. 28) ('It is only thanks to the illness that I have to agree that I belong existentially and socially to this category (of homosexuals)'). This remark illustrates that there is no sense of Aron's entertaining the concept of a homosexual community: he only concedes belonging to the category of homosexuals because he has AIDS-related illnesses.

Eight months after his interview in *Le Nouvel Observateur*, on 21 June 1998, Aron agreed to go on television to talk about 'Mon sida'.[42] This is to be seen again as a political gesture of visibility and an attempt at achieving social recognition of the reality of AIDS by means of a personal statement.

The front page of *Le Nouvel Observateur* had the following caption: 'Pour la première fois une personnalité brise le silence.' ('For the first time ever a well-known person breaks the silence.') The television programme is entitled, 'AIDS: After the confession'. The word 'aveu' in the title shows the same ambivalence as was noted earlier. But judging by the *tone* of the programme, it appears that the meaning of 'aveu' intended by the programme makers was always that of confession. And confession brings with it questions of guilt and repentance, with Catholic overtones. The television interviewer, Daniel Costelle, enquires about the circumstances of the 'Mon sida' interview in separate conversations with Aron and Schemla (he talks to the latter in her workplace rather than in Aron's apartment), and at times they both interview Aron in his apartment. In fact, as his introduction makes clear, Costelle is putting Aron and Schemla on trial ('When I saw in the kiosks this issue of *Le Nouvel Observateur* where he was *confessing* how and why he had been *struck by this terrible illness*: was it an act of exhibitionism? Has one got the right to do that? What is the responsibility of journalists?' [my emphasis]). Later on when questioning Schemla, he suggests that she had chosen to interview Aron for a scoop ('C'est un créneau que vous vous étiez choisi? On peut se poser cette question aussi...', 'Is it a niche you had chosen for yourself, one can also wonder...'), reflecting that AIDS sells newspapers.

It is difficult to understand Costelle's motives, unless one gives him credit for relaying the questions he thinks the public wants to ask, but he starts the interview with Schemla by asking her if she was not frightened of being contaminated when she went to interview someone that Le Pen calls a 'sidaïque'. When talking to Aron, he asks him if he has become plague-stricken since the original interview ('pestiféré') before stating that Le Pen's views are not as widespread as people think! He for one seems to be perpetuating such a discourse. Schemla also has her own agenda: when asked by Costelle what she thinks was important about Aron's original interview, she concentrates on one aspect exclusively, totally obliterating the fact that Aron is declaring his serological status and offering a testimony of living with AIDS: 'Il y a peu de gens qui, avec une telle simplicité, ont osé dire qu'être homo dans la société française d'aujourd'hui est un malheur existentiel.' ('Very few people, with such simplicity, have dared to say that being a homo[sexual] in French society today is an existential misfortune.') One can see how difficult it is for Aron not to lose the focus and accompanying tone of what *he* wants to communicate. Given what I have said above, 'aveu' does take the meaning of 'confession'.

There is no better illustration of this phenomenon than a section of the interview devoted to Costelle and Schemla interviewing Aron about guilt. They bring him back to the original interview where he had stated that he didn't feel guilty about the possibility that he might have contaminated someone else before learning he was HIV-positive. They explain that this is what shocked so many people and ask him again to justify the fact that he didn't have any *retrospective* remorse and to explain why he didn't try to have the test earlier. This echoes an earlier line of questioning from Costelle, who had asked him why he didn't try to get in touch with the American he thought had contaminated him once he knew he was HIV-positive. In the same vein, Schemla asks Aron if pointing the finger at someone – i.e., the American – is not a way of vindicating himself ('se disculper') in view of his past lifestyle. In this way, the guilt dimension is introduced and the misinformation that it is 'high-risk groups' (rather than 'high-risk sexual behaviours') that are passing on the virus is perpetuated. In his answer, Aron reminds them with regard to remorse that the main aim of the original interview was in fact to *exorcise such a feeling*. By implication, this is the clearest statement yet from Aron that he meant the word 'aveu' to mean 'admission'. The interviewers then expand on their questioning and ask if one can be happy as a homosexual. Aron replies

> Je ne pense pas qu'on puisse être heureux complètement. Il y a trop de réticences dites ou non dites dans le corps social, pour que le sujet concerné, l'homosexuel, n'éprouve pas cette mise à l'écart qui ne me paraît pas compatible avec le bonheur.

> I do not think that we can be completely happy. There is too much reticence, spoken or unspoken, in the social sphere, for the person concerned, the homosexual, not to feel this sidelining which does not seem to me to be compatible with happiness.

Schemla then asks him if he feels more at ease with his homosexuality now that he has made a public confession (!) – again Foucault's analysis evoked earlier is particularly pertinent. He replies that he does not know, but that since he now leads an extremely limited sex life, he does not feel *what she wants to make him say*. Aron is sending his interviewers the message that he is fully aware of their intention to make him admit something he does not agree with.

The main difference between the first interview and the second one is that Aron seems to be serene. Eight months have elapsed between the two. Schemla remarks that he is no longer angry, as he was in 'Mon sida', with politicians, the media and doctors. He states that, while

116

writing is the most important thing for him in life, on some days when he is feeling down, he wonders what the use of writing is and says that he has had enough and has nothing else left to say. He seems to have gone beyond his anger and to be staring death in the face: 'J'envisage la mort comme inéluctable et dans des délais relativement rapprochés.' ('I envisage death as inevitable and in a relatively short space of time.') Aron died in fact on 20 August 1988, less than two months after the television interview.

The main lesson to be learnt from this television programme is that the actual frameworks of discourse that are imposed upon Aron's own discourse of breaking the silence are guilt and shame. It is only if Aron is seen to express remorse (even if he himself uses the ambivalent term 'aveu', which could mean simply acceptance) that the fact of his being a homosexual who has developed AIDS is acceptable. And this has the effect of regulating homosexuality and of containing it within a discourse of unhappiness, perpetuating the hegemony of monogamous heterosexuality. There is also the underlying assumption that being a homosexual is synonymous with having AIDS.

To his credit, Aron resists such a 'confession', but it is difficult to disentangle his words from the framing of the questions by both interviewers. 'Speaking out' is not necessarily always 'breaking out'. So it is no surprise to learn that, as in the case of the original interview, Aron was misunderstood. Marsan reports that some homosexuals were unhappy with what he said. But as Marsan says, the 'damage' is done, not so much by Aron but by Schemla's statement – supposedly Aron's words – that very few people, with such simplicity, have dared to say that being a homosexual in French society today is an existential misfortune.[43] It is true that this is not exactly what Aron says. But Marsan's point is that this latter comment plays into the hands of the moral brigade, when in fact Aron was meditating about *his* life.[44] As analysed in the introduction, in France there had been next to nothing like a liberationist politics, and no theory of 'coming out', and Aron's position is linked to the history of homosexuality in France.[45] For people of Aron's generation, the discourse of *aveu* (as opposed to 'pride') must have seemed inevitable – and concomitantly the idea of homosexuality as synonymous with unhappiness. This is in marked contrast to the next generation spearheaded by Guy Hocquenghem in the late 1970s.

There is, however, a part of the programme which does under-mine the dominant discourse and which proves in itself the worth of Aron's original interview. At one point Schemla is being interviewed in her *Nouvel Observateur* office. She develops her idea that Aron had expressed the fact that homosexuality equals existential misfortune, which she now states as 'ce que nous vivons est intolérable quoique nous racontions' ('what we live through is unbearable whatever we say') – which is a gross misinterpretation of Aron's words. The assistant-director of the television programme suddenly appears in the frame. His name is Olivier, he is 30 (so he belongs to Hocquenghem's genera-tion, not Aron's) and he has known that he is HIV-positive for six months. He attributes the fact that he has decided to speak openly on television to Aron's original interview. He claims that it moved him and states that he is certain that he would not be speaking had Aron not led the way. This spontaneous action speaks volumes for the political gesture of Aron's 'Mon sida'. It is true that articulating the experience of HIV/AIDS and homosexuality on television runs against French constructions of the nationality/sexuality relationships. It can only be accepted if it is interpreted as a confession and ridden with guilt, whatever the original intentions of the author. But I would rather concentrate on the front page of *Le Nouvel Observateur* and the idea of 'breaking the silence'. Once someone breaks the silence, others will follow, as Olivier shows. Olivier chose to step to the other side of the camera and to speak.

Marsan develops the most crucial point when he writes that the polemic over Aron's declarations about homosexuality masked the true issue that he raised: 'En doutant de son bonheur passé, il voyait déjà l'issue absurde d'une vie. Ce qu'il tentait de dire, c'est l'horreur d'une telle lucidité.' ('In doubting his past happiness, he was already seeing the absurd end of a life. What he was trying to say is the horror of being so lucid.')[46] The tragedy of both 'Mon sida' and the television programme that followed is that this discursive mode of personal and political change was overlooked by the dominant discourse, but also by some PWAs and homosexuals.

In this chapter, we have seen two very different types of testimony, by two people belonging to different generations (to use the categories introduced in Chapter 1, Aron would belong to the Arcadia-type of homosexual and Simonin to those 'coming out' in the early 1980s). Despite all the forms of discrimination listed by Simonin, Aron states categorically during the television programme that discrimination, even nurses refusing to look after PWAs, is unheard of anywhere in France. Aron and Simonin are at opposite ends of the social scale: a French intellectual and a homeless person. And yet from another point of view their experiences were not dissimilar in trying to break the silence and to become visible. As Schemla puts it, 'Ce silence était un des blocages de la société française' ('This silence was one of the mental blocks of French society'). Break the silence they did. But at a cost, that of having the discourse of guilt, remorse and by implication recuperation/(re)construction substitute itself for their own voice, and very largely succeed. Early AIDS testimony appears to have been unable to evade altogether a narrative of guilty confession. This was perpetuated by the media culture of the time and also by the popular culture industry that produced the exploitative narratives of Part I, masking what is in fact a courageous attempt on both parts to be a witness.

5 Dreuilhe: Metaphor/Phantasy and Mobilisation

Corps à corps, Journal de Sida,[1] was published in France in 1987 by the prestigious publisher Gallimard in the series 'Au vif du sujet' ('At the heart of the matter') when Dreuilhe was 38. The book was published in North America in 1988. This text is characterised by what is referred to in the secondary literature as 'the military metaphor'. *Corps à corps* has been caught up in the wider debate about the merits or drawbacks of using this metaphor for AIDS writing.

Let me start by describing the metaphoric texture of *Corps à corps*. AIDS is represented as World War Three, involving 165 countries (p. 28), compared to a tank destroying everything in its path, rolling over all the defences put up by modern medicine, ignoring any cry for mercy and oblivious to the crushing of the limbs it drives over (p. 42). Dreuilhe refers to himself as a civilian whose life was shattered when he was mobilised by AIDS (pp. 14–15). Lymphocytes are massed on the border while lavish pleasure (the pre-AIDS gay scene) has reduced the T4 cell count, the main defence of the Maginot Line.[2] It all started with border skirmishes (flu, bronchitis) which were ignored (p. 23), as when the Popular Front in France ignored Hitler's intentions. The

120

specificity of AIDS is that it reinvents guerrilla warfare, using psychological warfare (p. 137) and PWAs, if they are to stand a chance, must engage in this type of war (p. 17). The body is invaded by the HIV virus and the gay community is likened to Troy (pp. 143, 149), welcoming the fatal horse with open arms (the liberalisation of sexuality saw an increase in multiple sexual partners and unprotected sex, and hence facilitated HIV infection); indeed a whole section is entitled 'Le cheval de Troie' (pp. 36–54) ('The Trojan Horse'). Medical treatment with AZT is likened to V-2 missile bombardments on the enemy (p. 40). The only difference between AIDS and war (though the narrator questions whether it is really a difference) is that PWAs are dying for no reason, whereas in war there is supposed to be a cause worth fighting for (p. 48).

Presented as an 'AIDS diary', *Corps à corps* is not a *diary* in the traditional sense of the term. There are no dated entries, and the book is divided into twelve sections, all connected to the 'military metaphor',[3] with no specific chronology within these sections. In fact, the English translation of the title omits any reference to 'journal/diary': *Mortal Embrace: Living with AIDS*.[4] *Corps à corps* is narrated in the first person by a man who identifies himself as the author of the book, Alain Emmanuel Dreuilhe, and presents himself as being gay and HIV-positive, having developed AIDS-related illnesses.[5] His partner (called 'Oliver' in the book) has just died; he was also HIV-positive.[6] Having lost Oliver in the span of three months (p. 57) (a period described as a blitzkrieg) and finding himself alone and near to despair (with the feeling that the enemy was dropping propaganda leaflets telling him to surrender too, p. 40), he starts to write a diary for the first time in his life in order to have a companion.[7] The illness is referred to as a mental illness, not so much because the virus can attack the brain, but because it forces PWAs into isolation and anguish and therefore alienation (p. 14).[8] Later on in the text the narrator comments that through writing, that most *solitary* of acts, he sensed the true plight of a whole *generation* (p. 123). This shift from the individual to the collective will be one of the key characteristics of his text.

The action takes place in New York where Dreuilhe has lived for the last decade, working as a translator. So we can see at the outset that his experience will be different from that of the French PWAs, because he is living in the United States, even though he is not American and must have felt he was a foreigner. He describes having been ill for the last three years. We have seen that the book develops into a long 'military metaphor'. AIDS is the enemy attacking Private Dreuilhe's body and resistance is organised warfare. This process corresponds to what Danthe calls psychological techniques of visualisation, which are supposed to encourage the immune system to start *fighting* infection[9] (notice how difficult it is for me not to employ military metaphors). In this scenario, the PWA is no longer a passive victim but becomes an active agent who can call on resources so as not to give in to the virus. The latter is identified as a visible target to be aimed at and loses in the process some of its aura of invulnerability, redressing the balance of power. And this is certainly Dreuilhe's aim: 'Mon espoir inconscient est que ce livre, surgi comme une excroissance cancéreuse, hors de mon cerveau, devienne un appendice monstrueux qu'il sera possible de séparer finalement de mon corps' (p. 178) ('My unconscious hope is that this book, sprung from my brain like a cancerous growth, will become a monstrous appendage easily excised from my body', p. 139). The 'military metaphor' runs throughout the book, and it could be conceived of as a shield whose function is to protect Dreuilhe by fiction-alising his life situation. The distancing process might also have the effect of hindering communication with readers who may react negatively to its extended use. We saw above that Dreuilhe described himself as a civilian before he was mobilised. Photographs of him show a very sensitive and gentle face, slightly feminine, and the combination of unmilitary 'softness' and military 'hardness' intensify the poignancy of Dreuilhe's representation. In fact, he mentions at the beginning of *Corps à corps* having been a deserter for a long time and having avoided conscription into the French army, an act more in keeping with the vulnerability his photographs suggest (p. 19).[10]

Dreuilhe is deeply ambivalent in his relationship to AIDS: though wanting to extricate it from his body (as in the last quotation), he also paradoxically calls it 'mon dernier amour' (p. 14) ('my last love', p. 6)[11] and writes that he finds it romantic (p. 77). Elsewhere he confesses, 'Il y a forcément amour entre nous puisqu'il y a eu jalousie' (p. 189) ('There must be love between us, because there once was jealousy', p. 149), explaining in a courageous piece of writing how he was jealous of his partner Oliver's AIDS which was more spectacular than the progression of his own illness. *Corps à corps* is presented as a love letter to AIDS, with the ambiguity of being both weapon and white flag (p. 189). The clashing juxtaposition of the infantryman image with the physical appearance of Dreuilhe can be reconciled in light of this ambiguity. *Corps à corps* can also signify a hand-to-hand *embrace* (*Mortal Embrace* being the title chosen for the English translation) in which case Dreuilhe would be referring to sexual encounters. The French title evokes more powerfully a violent struggle, and the English title an intimate act leading to Thanatos.[12] These are not mutually exclusive.

I intend my reading to enter the debate around the 'military metaphor', but first of all I am aware that the book has been generally read one-dimensionally, and I want to start by appreciating its composite richness. Following Murray Pratt, I want to read the text with a sense of respect, bearing in mind that very often a reintegration of a sense of self is the greatest victory possible in AIDS writing.

Wetsel states that *Corps à corps* 'is quintessentially French in style and sensibility',[13] with many allusions to Proust. Indeed *À la recherche du temps perdu* contains many observations about the Great War which Dreuilhe applies to his situation (p. 45) and he describes AIDS as his Albertine ('ennemi terrifiant et familier, comme un démon ou un génie', p. 15 ('a frightful, intimate enemy, like a demon or familiar spirit', p. 7)); again one notes the ambiguity towards AIDS. There are also nods to other writers such as Barthes[14] with the odd reference to Kafka's *Metamorphosis* (p. 60). The text also contains a good deal of humour,[15] including parodies of classical lines[16] and also self-irony.[17] Dreuilhe is positioning himself within the French literary tradition. Throughout the text, there are many allusions to Greek mythology, and the odd one to Shakespeare (p. 52). But Dreuilhe is wary of producing 'literature'. He believes that words dilute his perception of AIDS as possessing violent strength. He is equally aware that his text is not a war memoir like those of De Gaulle or Churchill because he is only a foot soldier (pp. 177–78; also p. 186). It is also interesting to note that he uses the term 'art engagé' (p. 178) ('committed art/literature') to describe *Corps à corps*.

Dreuilhe believes that it is only if one can stand back from an event that one gains the necessary perspective to give a useful rendering of it, including communicating feelings. But he is immersed in the war, positioned on the front line, and time is running out (p. 178). Throughout the text, time moves at a fast pace with hours representing days and months years (p. 191), the illness providing what Dreuilhe eloquently calls 'un raccourci de l'existence, qui en est aussi une amère parodie' (p. 191) ('an abridged version of existence that is also a bitter parody', p. 151).[18] And inevitably, AIDS brings on a confrontation with death, which PWAs were not expecting in their thirties but in their seventies (p. 126). This fact is all the more difficult to bear since when Dreuilhe narrates the agony of his partner, his analysis is that the last stages of the illness created a barrier between them, and that Oliver died alone. Dreuilhe is therefore under no illusions, he knows that he will die alone too. Suddenly he realises that to mourn for Oliver is a way of mourning for himself (p. 58). Writing the death of Oliver equals writing his own death.[19] Tragically, Thanatos could interrupt his writing at any time so he has to write as quickly as possible (p. 179).

I would now like to draw attention to an interview Dreuilhe gave in Montreal to accompany the publication of his book. In *Corps à corps*, the narrator states that it was during his psychoanalysis that the warrior metaphors came to him; he used them to express that he felt he was fighting alone while the civilians (HIV-negative people) lived as before; this made him both bitter and determined to stay alive (pp. 42–43). In the interview, Dreuilhe explains that the analyst, a woman who specialises in working with PWAs, encouraged him to develop military metaphors after he had referred to his doctor as a general. 'Elle me dit: "C'est intéressant, pourquoi ne mettez-vous pas cela par écrit, *pour qu'on en parle?*"' (my emphasis) ('She said to me: "This is interesting, why don't you write all this down, *so that we can talk about it?*"').[20] He proceeded to do so and states that the act of writing about it released him totally from the need to talk to her about it. He felt much better and was not interested in repeating to her what he had already written down; the psychoanalysis carried on along conventional lines (his family, his relationship to Oliver). Dreuilhe concludes,

> Mon rapport n'est pas très fort avec cette thérapeute, c'est presqu'un rapport agacé. Ce rapport a souffert en outre du fait qu'elle ne voyait pas ce que j'écrivais et que je ne lui en parlais pas; qu'il y a tout un univers de mon inconscient qui lui échappe totalement. Elle fait quand même partie des autres! (Rires)

> My relationship to my therapist is not very strong, it is almost a fraught relationship. This relationship has also suffered from the fact that she was not reading what I was writing and I was not talking to her about it; the fact that there is a whole world of my unconscious that escapes her totally. After all she too is one of the others! (Laughter)

A few things need to be unpacked from the above comments. The analyst suggests that he should write the metaphors down so that *they can talk about it*, as a way of deepening their therapeutic relationship; but he deliberately decides to keep this information from her, admitting that it has had the effect of hindering their relationship. His comment that 'she too is one of the others' presumably alludes to the fact that the therapist is HIV-negative, and unlikely to understand what he is going through. He seems quite jubilant about this as the interview records laughter: he has played a trick on her and is proud of it. There is no way of knowing which school of therapy his therapist (named in his acknowledgements as Natalie Becker) belonged to, but one can safely assume that Dreuilhe is following a Freudian psychoanalysis.

I propose to read *Corps à corps* as the *hidden* part of the therapy, or rather the part hidden from the therapist but shown to us readers. We are effectively positioned as therapists, being given the missing part of the puzzle which is deliberately withheld from Becker. This is consistent with my psychoanalytic approach, one of the three techniques utilised throughout this book. For my main theoretical tool, I will rely on Graham Dawson's *Soldier Heroes*,[21] itself heavily influenced by Melanie Klein, referring specifically to the second chapter, 'Masculinity, Phantasy and History'.

Dreuilhe explains the reason behind his use of the military metaphor in a passage where he exclaims that he really wants to demystify and exorcise AIDS, just as a soldier must see the human being behind the invincible aura of the enemy (p. 52). During an interview on French national television on a literary programme called 'Apostrophes' in autumn 1987, Dreuilhe said that when he started his book, it was in order to show AIDS that he was not frightened of it. Another possible motivation for his turning to metaphor is that, in this particular case, it creates a necessary distance so as to write about AIDS: hence perhaps unable to bear writing that he is losing both eyes to the cytomegalovirus which signifies the onset of blindness, Dreuilhe uses instead the allegory of France losing the two provinces Alsace and Lorraine to Germany. Using such distancing techniques is a difficult balancing act, for there is a danger of actually detaching from one's emotions, or splitting in psychoanalytical terms, and this is something which I will examine further.

Following Dawson, I prefer to substitute the term 'phantasy' for 'metaphor'. *Fantasy* refers to imaginative forms; *phantasy* also includes unconscious processes. It is 'an ongoing process, a kind of narrative'[22] where both psychic and social dimensions are present. It crosses the boundaries between the 'real' and the 'unconscious'. Dreuilhe extends his military phantasy to society at large. Hence the enemy is defined, not so much as the HIV virus, but as the media, public opinion, his father, all his friends and allies, as well as partly himself, those who say and believe that AIDS is incurable and fatal (p. 16). My use of the term 'phantasy' is technical. I understand that the ravages inflicted by the HIV virus on Dreuilhe's mind and on his body are so threatening to his sense of self that he has to put up the most vigorous defence he is capable of; he needs to mobilise all of his resources into this military phantasy in order to survive psychically. All the more so since he believes that socially he is alone in the world because of a total lack of external solidarity. There is also a distinction between military and militaristic, the latter not necessarily following from the former, and Dreuilhe never crosses this boundary.

'The self's defensive responses are shaped by the need to maintain composure in social as well as psychic life.'[23] The phantasy is therefore extended to society. We saw above that Dreuilhe's first use of the military phantasy was to express how he felt he was fighting alone while those behind the lines lived as before. This makes of *Corps à corps* a testimony to the political apathy surrounding the AIDS crisis in the mid-1980s. Dreuilhe uses the powerful image of the Holocaust, an image used not uncontroversially by American writers at the time. Hence, he compares himself to Anne Frank writing her diary (p. 60), the hospital uniform of PWAs becomes the striped pyjamas, the uniform of POWs (p. 4) and the indifference of the German petty bourgeoisie watching their Jewish neighbours being taken away is equated to that of the heterosexual population watching their homosexual neighbours taken away by the illness (p. 49). He also uses the image of the Occupation in France during the Second World War. For the time being, the enemy has the upper hand but the Resistance is getting organised. The tactic is to play for time until the landing in Normandy of the American scientists, especially as 'nos corps sont territoires occupés et seule une résolution farouche permet de ne pas perdre l'espoir' (p. 27) ('our bodies are occupied territories, and only fierce resolution keeps us from losing all hope', p. 17). I sense in this sentence immense desperation: either Dreuilhe lies down and dies, or he invents the military phantasy; indeed, he talks at times of deserting, as when his intestinal war breaks out again (p. 69). During the television programme, he describes using metaphors as a way of reassuring himself.

Melanie Klein explains the processes of social as well as psychic composure by the fact that 'self-composure is always established on the basis of an imaginative positioning of others: as they are drawn into the internal psychic world, and allotted parts in the narrative phantasies that are played out within it'.[24] This is where we find a creative leap in Dreuilhe's positioning of others. We saw that at the beginning of his psychoanalysis he was comparing his doctor to a general (which prompted his analyst to ask him to elaborate on this by writing it down). From there it is a short step to setting up in his phantasy world a whole army fighting alongside him, united in one cause: defeating the enemy. He needs to believe that he is not fighting alone, for he knows that he would be defeated: the odds are too over-whelmingly stacked against him. Even an imaginary readership is drawn into *Corps à corps*: 'Chacun de mes lecteurs deviendrait un de mes soldats' (p. 178) ('Each of my readers would become one of my soldiers').

Dreuilhe is too guarded, as can be gleaned from some passages, for him not to *know* somewhere inside himself that his way of making sense of his status as a PWA[25] is a phantasy. He needs to protect this phantasy from outside assaults, for personal disintegration would surely follow. If we now return to the question of why Dreuilhe chose not to share his writing with his analyst, it seems relevant to this issue. As Dawson writes: 'In analysis, interest is directed through the manifest form of imagos [imaginative figures], towards the unconscious phan-tasies underlying projective investments in them'.[26] In a way, it is much safer for Dreuilhe to confide his text to readers whose interpretation need not concern him, than to his psychoanalyst. Indeed, he reports in the text his analyst telling him that the thrill of excitement which only danger can provide (the very situation he is describing to her, p. 39) is a characteristic of narcissism (p. 188). This makes him wonder whether he takes himself to be a hero writing his 'autohagiography', to which he responds that in fact he is in dialogue *with* AIDS: 'Je m'adresse au SIDA lui-même [...] pour lui faire savoir [...] que je ne me – et ne le – laisserai pas faire [...]' (p. 188) ('I address AIDS itself [...] to let it be known to AIDS [...] that I will not let it get the better of me [...]'). He writes to AIDS, the God of War, in order to be spared.

Since the military phantasy is essential to his survival, he cannot afford psychically for Becker to take his defences apart. This is perhaps the greatest merit of *Corps à corps*. Dreuilhe is going along with psycho-analysis but also substituting for it his own way of coping with AIDS. He believes the military 'phantasy' to be the best defence against disintegration. And what he is doing by writing and publishing his book is offering it to other HIV-positive people and PWAs (p. 186) as a way of empowering what he calls his 'compagnons de lutte' (p. 186) ('brothers-in-arms', p. 146). Even the fact of his death will become an act of witness. In Chambers's analysis, 'The death of the PWA, whether as an author or no, has already the sense of an act of witness and constitutes a mode of address "for others", one that the writing of a diary only amplifies and specifies.'[27]

Dreuilhe also records witnessing the death of his partner, Oliver, mainly in the section entitled 'À la recherche de l'allié perdu' (pp. 55–65) ('Hope recaptured'). I was touched by the following image: the military phantasy is fine-tuned into a nuclear war followed by an atomic winter, with their isolation rendered as the three of them (including Oliver's mother Julia) stuck in a space capsule (p. 57). What functions for an author as a phenomenon of distancing may well have an involving effect for the reader: this nuclear winter landscape is evocative enough to transcribe the utter devastation of the experience to the reader. We are then told that Oliver unplugged the machines that kept him alive, perhaps to save his lover who was getting weaker himself through looking after him (p. 59). One can guess that Dreuilhe is experiencing survivor's guilt.

Over the last few paragraphs, I have been building up a picture of *Corps à corps* as a political gesture, part of what I referred to in my introduction as the literature of commitment of the 1980s. Dreuilhe himself referred to his book as 'art engagé' (p. 178) ('committed art/literature'). Indeed, the opening paragraph of the text makes the point that everyone else has talked about AIDS except PWAs, who have had their voices muffled by the so-called experts (p. 11). Elsewhere he writes that everything said or heard in the media about PWAs appeared to him to be false (p. 59), and that if PWAs don't fight, they will be the last homosexuals, which is something Le Pen and his affiliates are hoping for (p. 187). Dreuilhe's appearance on the literary programme 'Apostrophes' to talk about his book is also a political gesture.

Discrimination is rife, and this text serves as a witness to this, reminding us of conditions in the mid-1980s. In hospital, Dreuilhe is asked to wear a mask so as not to breathe out the virus (p. 105), nurses wear gloves and masks when they deal with PWAs, and there are little red labels on their notes reading 'Precautions –AIDS' (p. 107).[28] All this, added to the fact that few people are authorised to visit PWAs, makes Dreuilhe compare a stay in hospital to the situation of soldiers in the trenches because of the isolation and of the quarantine conditions they live in (p. 103). He has to beg and plead for his dentist to keep him as a patient since others may flee the practice if they know the dentist treats an HIV-positive person (p. 132). Funeral parlours systematically cremate all PWAs (p. 43). Dreuilhe reports a heterosexual doctor who treats PWAs telling him that he feels more closely involved with a white homosexual PWA 'from a good background' than with a black drug addict, which is bound to have an impact on the quality of care and treatment (p. 33). Dreuilhe denounces the danger of setting up the binary 'good/bad' in relation to PWAs.

But the army is not united. Dreuilhe courageously highlights the fact that there are clear divisions between what he describes as typical PWAs (black, often socially deprived heterosexual drug addicts) and mostly white homosexual lawyers, teachers, students, sales executives and white-collar workers. The situation is reminiscent for him of the Vietnam war with its forgotten black soldiers; now as then, the media focuses on the suffering of white middle-class Americans as the acceptable face of society (pp. 31–33). This shows ample evidence of hierarchical masculinities. There is also self-sabotage at work. Dreuilhe talks about HIV-positive people who have not gone on to develop AIDS as walking time-bombs (p. 44), an army marching towards itself. Dreuilhe is raising the issue of responsibilities.

Dreuilhe is aware that what he calls conscientious objectors will criticise the way he has militarised the conflict and blame his latent 'neofascism'; others will say that, in the context of the military, courage has no value (pp. 186–87). This seems to be an appropriate point at which to tackle the general debate around books such as *Corps à corps*. In the red corner is Susan Sontag with *AIDS and its Metaphors*; Sontag wants

> to see retired [...] the military metaphor [because of] [...] the effect of the military imagery on thinking about sickness and health [...] it overmobilizes, it overdescribes, and it powerfully contributes to the

excommunicating and stigmatizing of the ill [...] We are not being invaded. The body is not a battlefield. The ill are neither unavoidable casualties nor the enemy. We – medicine, society – are not authorized to fight back by any means whatever ...'[29]

In the blue corner is D.A. Miller. He starts by making the point that Sontag's recommendation that military metaphors of illness be 'retired' is itself a violent act since there is violence in forced retirement, before continuing, 'Unwilling to specify which war metaphors are particularly demoralizing to people with AIDS, Sontag characteristically rejects them all [...]'.[30] For Miller, some military metaphors are useful in terms of resisting AIDS through 'militancy' and AIDS activism. Slogans such as 'Fight back, fighting AIDS', and organisations such as 'Mobilisation against AIDS' empower PWAs. Finally, he concludes, 'It is almost unspeakably insulting to suggest that "fighting AIDS" sooner or later means fighting people with AIDS [...] her text makes a last recommendation that would deny [PWAs] the right to speak of themselves – polemically, militantly, in any voice but that of victims [...]'.[31]

Broqua has shown, using the field of memory, that military metaphors and references to wars are privileged instances of the opposition between national and illegitimate or underground memories. Broqua cites three examples of these: a poster showing an image of soldiers and the legend, 'In fifty years, we will not have veterans: ACT-UP Paris at war against AIDS'; World Women's Day saw some women going to the Arc de Triomphe and lying down below a banner reading 'To the unknown HIV-positive woman'; on 11 November 1996, during the annual military parade commemorating the First World War armistice, militants unfolded a banner showing Jacques Chirac with the following question: 'How many dead from AIDS has he buried?'[32] It seems undeniable that these 'metaphors' are actually empowering for PWAs and ACT-UP Paris militants. And it is indeed difficult to reconcile these examples with Sontag's argument.

An interesting dimension to the debate, which has hardly been touched upon in the secondary literature, is the gendered nature of the 'military metaphors' – though women readers have the ability to phantasise as much as their male counterparts, a fact that I am not disputing. In *Corps à corps*, the war is men's business. Women are there as support for comforting the soldiers; as soldiers' mothers (p. 188), often ashamed to tell the truth about their son's illness for fear of having to admit that they are either homosexuals or drug addicts (p. 47); or as mourners (*Stabat Mater*, p. 31). Dreuilhe himself broaches this issue when he writes that if unconsciously he started by comparing the epidemic to war, it is because it concerned men. As he is writing, he agrees that more and more women and children are being afflicted. But, according to him, women are presented by the media as victims of men who have infected them, a type of civilian casualty; personally, he thinks that they wish to remain neutral like Switzerland (p. 31). And of course Dreuilhe's therapist, to whom he refuses to show his writing, is a woman.

There are two strands to the military metaphor debate: the public and the private. In terms of the private sphere (and this is where my use of the term 'phantasy' rather than 'metaphor' might hopefully advance the debate), concentrating on Dreuilhe, one can see how the use of the phantasy encompasses both the psychic and the social, and that even private metaphors have social implications. This in turn makes Sontag's argument weaker. In the process of writing, a kind of identification takes place for Dreuilhe 'with an idealization of what the self would like to become and has discovered',[33] and this is the way he has chosen to survive. I am not claiming that Dreuilhe is an infantry-man waiting to appear. On the contrary: he is in danger of feeling totally overwhelmed because of the 'disintegrating effects of anxiety'[34] caused by AIDS and he therefore needs to put up defences. He has to visualise these defences as inner and outer, projecting an imagined solidarity with the whole world. This shows the apathy of governments in reacting to the AIDS crisis, both in the United States and in France, and the devastating effect it had on PWAs but also their extraordinary resourcefulness. Like Simonin with the avalanche metaphor, Dreuilhe is struggling to feel empowered, having to imagine through figuration a sense that society has joined him in his battle against AIDS.

Let us not forget that the events narrated in the book probably took place in 1985–86, which is the point of juncture between what Weeks characterises as the second and third periods in the AIDS pandemic (the period of moral panic and the time when governments started to take the illness seriously). Symbolically, Dreuilhe's book belongs to the *literature of mobilisation*. In his study 'The Language of War in AIDS Discourse', Michael Sherry writes that the language of war was ubiquitous in the discourse on AIDS during the 1980s and that it seemed to be dissipating by the early 1990s.[35] Quite a few books were published in America using the military metaphor. Sherry convincingly demonstrates how this is specific to America and rooted in its history of conflicts. He also mentions Dreuilhe's book to show that it is not a uniquely American phenomenon.[36] One could argue that Dreuilhe had lived in New York for ten years, and that therefore he was imbued with American culture if not its history of conflicts.

What a lot of North American commentators may not have been aware of is the fact that Dreuilhe had lived in proximity to military conflicts throughout his childhood: he grew up with civil war in Cairo, surrounded by Nasser's tanks, then lived through the Indochinese war (Cambodia, Vietnam). Significantly, references to these events pepper the text.[37] In a straightforward reading, this could explain the origin of the military phantasy. But it would be too easy a reading. In the 'Apostrophes' interview, the interviewer actually asked Dreuilhe if the war metaphor came to him because of his childhood experiences and exposure. Dreuilhe replied that he had never put these two facts together (which indeed of itself proves nothing). He says that in his book he tried to avoid talking about his personal history, and only did so when it had a connection with his illness: 'Je voulais me présenter comme une entité collective dont je serais une sorte de porte-parole.'[38] ('I wanted to present myself as a collective entity of which I would be a kind of spokesperson.') An *individual* choosing the term '*collective entity*' seems to refer to the literature of mobilisation.

Analysing the reception of *Corps à corps*, Wetsel shows how it 'stands in a no-man's-land somewhere between France and America. American readers, unused to French rhetorical tradition, perhaps misunderstood Dreuilhe's truthfully courageous vision. French readers (particularly gay ones) have been mystified and even offended by Dreuilhe's brilliant and extended martial metaphor.'[39] This shows that being positioned between two cultures can sometimes have the effect of one's being misconstrued by both of them. What happened to Dreuilhe echoes Aron's misadventures in being criticised both for 'Mon sida' and for the subsequent television programme, when in fact Aron and Dreuilhe were both trying to testify publicly about the reality of being a PWA. But this positioning can also have advantages. As Wetsel remarks, Dreuilhe's take on the AIDS crisis could not be less French. Using Guibert as a contrast, Wetsel points to how Dreuilhe really shows a sense of the gay community in the United States, this sense of community being sadly lacking in France in the 1980s.

Dreuilhe explains the title *Corps à corps* as follows: the outer defences (the social) have failed PWAs and the enemy has reached individuals; the only thing left is hand-to-hand combat with cold steel.[40] Having been let down by society – which did not stop the enemy – PWAs can count only on their individual courage and personal resources (p. 30). Dreuilhe has little time for Fritz Zorn and his book about cancer, *Mars*,[41] since he is judged to have kept his diary ('journal') *as a pacifist*. This confirms my analysis about the specificity of Dreuilhe's diary in shifting from the individual to the collective. *Corps à corps* could signify a *hand-to-hand combat* with the social as well as with the biological body.

It may be appropriate at this stage to go back to the generic conventions of *Corps à corps*. We saw that it is presented as a diary, but lacks the conventions of diary entries, since it consists of twelve sections all linked to the military metaphor, and with no chronology. It resembles more a type of autobiographical writing, but this label would not do justice to the committed aspect of the text with its metaphorics of mobilisation. Delvaux rightly describes the text as an autobiographical discourse, but one that includes a social and a public discourse, further elucidating,

> Le texte de Dreuilhe est certes une auto-narration du sida, un 'journal', mais c'est en tant qu'il se situe à un carrefour du 'je' autobiographique, du

discours historique et d'un discours social contemporain du moment de l'écriture [...][42]

Dreuilhe's text is indeed an AIDS self-narrative, a 'diary', but only in as much as it is positioned at the crossroads between the autobiographical 'I', historical discourse and a contemporary social discourse of the time of writing [...]

She argues that Dreuilhe's text puts into question the status of auto-biographical discourse as solipsistic. Hence Delvaux keeps the label diary ('journal') for *Corps à corps* but widens its definition from private diary to everyday experience ('le quotidien'), and to Dreuilhe's formula of the 'journal-tract' (diary-tract).[43] One can see now more clearly how Dreuilhe transforms a genre, traditionally reserved for an *individual* experience (the diary), into a *collective* uprising. This tinkering with genres shows the difficulties inherent in trying to represent an experience previously unknown (being a PWA) that is either misunderstood or mis-recognised by society, and in turn by literature, given that the experience is understood *not to be amenable* to the conventional repre-sentations, which are the only ones available. It also shows the ingenuity of Dreuilhe. His recourse to the military metaphor is readable as an attempt to make available, through figuration, his own sense, as a PWA, of being embattled – embattled physically and biomedically, but also socially. One thing is certain: like the work of Simonin and Aron, *Corps à corps* is part of AIDS testimony.

I think there is enough evidence to assume that 'going to war' is an appropriate metaphor, or rather phantasy. In discussing phantasies in the Kleinian sense, Dawson takes as his starting point the concept of 'psychic imagos' (imaginative figures) and, in order to draw the cultural into this concept, he creates the notion of 'cultural imaginaries', which he takes to mean 'vast networks of interlinking discursive themes, images, motifs and narrative forms that are publicly available within a culture at any one time, and articulate its psychic and social dimen-sions';[44] in other words, this is the function that the avalanche served for Simonin. In *Corps à corps*, AIDS is constructed as the enemy which the individual body and the whole social body must get rid of. The military phantasy seems one of the best options available in the 1980s to write about AIDS in an effort to try to mobilise one's own resources as well as those of the whole of society. After all, one does not mobilise people to go to war with a language of peace. In the social context of the time, it makes sense for Dreuilhe to try to convince each reader to become engaged in the fight against AIDS. As Lévy and Nouss write,

> La maladie se métaphorise quand une société donnée en a besoin et elle se met à signifier en fonction de ce besoin [...] pour les sidéens, face à une médicalisation qui apparaît majoritairement répressive et un discours social les stigmatisant, la maladie devient une identité qui illustre le refus de cette oppression.[45]

> Illness becomes a metaphor when a given society needs it and it starts to signify according to this need [...] for PWAs, faced with a health care system that is mostly repressive and a social discourse that stigmatises them, illness becomes an identity that symbolises the refusal of this oppression.

The main advantage of cultural imaginaries is that they 'furnish public forms which both organize knowledge of the social world and give shape to phantasies within the apparently "internal" domain of psychic life'.[46] This reads like a copybook definition of what Dreuilhe is trying to achieve with *Corps à corps*. Hence the military phantasy corresponds to 'cultural imaginaries' and provides Dreuilhe with a way of not fragmenting internally as well as with a cultural referent to reach out to other people, where he can manufacture for himself a *figural*[47] sense of solidarity with the outside world waging the same war as him.[48] This represents the originality of his work. He also avoids, and is the first author to do so, the 'just punishment' narrative imposed on all AIDS fiction studied in Part I, and superimposed on the AIDS testimonies of Aron and Simonin.

I now want to assess the impact of Dreuilhe's phantasy in the text and as the text draws to a close. I need to formulate this problem differently. Couched in Kleinian psychoanalytic terms, we can ask: how far does he achieve a sense of composure ('a more integrated self, open to its own contradictions and more tolerant of painful experience, confronts and strives to transform its anxieties, in efforts to reconcile the conflicting imagos'),[49] or does he reach a more 'defensive mode enabled by psychic splitting [...] based on a denial of destructive and painful aspects of its own experience and of the anxieties to which these give rise'?[50] Essentially, one expects both psychic states to be present, each being the condition of the other.

Using the Kleinian schema, phantastical object relations (the latter concept meaning one's sense of relatedness to the social environment) can be identified in *Corps à corps*. I have mentioned the gendered nature of the debate around the military metaphor as well as the gendered nature of its repudiation, and this is relevant here. There is a splitting between the feminised self and the masculinised self which Dreuilhe consistently calls the 'martial' side (etymologically, 'martial' comes from Mars, the God of War – as we saw, Dreuilhe says that his book is a letter asking the God of War to spare him, p. 188). He takes his lead from his doctor who is described as using 'martial speech' when he tells Dreuilhe, among other things, to grit his teeth. The latter concludes that he has just had a real pep talk, reminiscent of Napoleon addressing the troops before Austerlitz (pp. 61–62). He derives a certain pride from also adopting this attitude: 'Je dois reconnaître qu'il m'arrive de jouir de l'admiration que suscite chez mes proches mon attitude martiale' (p. 79) ('I admit that I sometimes enjoy the admiration my martial attitude arouses in those close to me', p. 57). This attitude is used as a yardstick and Dreuilhe confides that he judges other PWAs according to martial criteria (p. 25). AIDS, or rather one of the side-effects of the drugs (diarrhoea), is seen as feminising the body: 'Les écoulements féminisent toujours inconsciemment, ce qui nuit à l'image martiale que j'essaie d'avoir de moi' (pp. 69–70) ('Discharges are always unconsciously feminizing, which doesn't help the martial image I try to have of myself', p. 49). The flip side of a 'martial attitude' is sheer *terror* – elsewhere *Corps à corps* is described as a witnessing of his terror (p. 189); so we can see how close Dreuilhe is to fragmenting. His martial attitude is a defence mechanism typical of some constructions of masculinity. Talking about a PWA who is scared, he comments,

'Malgré son intelligence et sa sensibilité, il n'avait pas encore l'esprit martial qui aurait pu le libérer de sa *terreur* manifeste' (my emphasis, p. 127) ('Despite his obvious intelligence and sensitivity, he hadn't yet adopted the martial spirit that might have released him from his obvious *terror*'). Dreuilhe is displaying an iron body when he knows that his body is falling apart. The 'martial spirit', synonymous with 'militancy', is also applied to women. Hence when his wife is asked by an inquisitive Dutch camera crew how she feels about watching him die, he comments, 'Elle a martialement répondu que je vis avec le SIDA, que je n'en meurs pas et qu'elle est là pour m'aider à le vivre' (p. 156) ('She answered martially, replying that I am not dying of AIDS, but living with it, and that she is there to help me live with it'). A 'martial' spirit is the key strategic defence. So at this stage, because of his splitting (masculine/feminine), it appears that Dreuilhe is showing signs of 'denial of destructive and painful aspects of his own experience and of the anxieties to which these give rise'.[51] He is defending himself against his own vulnerability. On an inner level, psychic reintegration would effectively mean that one integrates one's fears and anxieties, including one's vulnerability, masculine/feminine side, and sheer terror as well as what Dreuilhe calls the 'martial' attitude. But in fact these binaries continue to coexist towards the end of the text, especially as death approaches.

The function of this splitting is not to be read negatively. It provides Dreuilhe with a respite thanks to his military phantasy, and this is where I think that *Corps à corps* is innovative. By-passing psychoanalysis, Dreuilhe finds a way, through writing, using the military phantasy which echoes cultural imaginaries, to mobilise his energies to fight the disease, and in the process to send out a message of hope and militancy. This is done at a time when there had been general apathy and disengagement (but not among those affected), and when a literature of mobilisation was necessary as well as general mobilisation. Dreuilhe is perhaps the only one to have imagined forms of solidarity that might have encouraged a collective response.

In the acknowledgements which are posted at the end of the book, Dreuilhe writes that he has shifted from anger to compassion, from revolt to serenity, and in the process transcended sorrow and self-pity

(p. 162). So it looks as if the military phantasy has engendered a sense of compassion and serenity and diffused the necessary first stage of anger and revolt. Even when he compares himself and other PWAs to freedom fighters, Dreuilhe states that their common aim is to glorify freedom, health and peace and to reject constraint, illness and war (p. 174).[52]

The writing process helps to bring on a sense of reintegration by its reflexive nature: 'Plus que ma thérapie, l'écriture m'a fait comprendre la complexité des sentiments que ma situation faisait naître en moi' (p. 185) ('Writing, even more than my psychotherapy, has helped me to understand the complexity of feeling this situation arouses in me', p. 145). Ultimately, writing has made him less afraid (p. 123). In this respect, Dreuilhe has completed a journey parallel to that of Juliette, Winer, Simonin and Aron. Dreuilhe believes he has invented *his* figural way of coping with AIDS, 'Car il est certainement magique que l'aggravation de ma maladie se soit suspendue depuis que j'ai entrepris ce journal' (p. 185) ('Because it's certainly magical that my condition has stopped deteriorating since I began writing this diary').[53] There is bound to be some self-deceit involved in this statement. But the important factor is that Dreuilhe *believes* it, or portrays himself as believing it in *Corps à corps*.

Dreuilhe has found a new sense of composure thanks to the writing process. Socially, the military phantasy has enabled him to build a sense of solidarity and therefore to survive psychically; it also serves as a political message. He writes openly that even if he ends up dying of AIDS, he is no longer frightened of it because the writing has purified him, giving a meaning to the last three years of care, grief and mourning. That meaning is encapsulated in the following statement: 'Je serai mort pour une cause à laquelle je n'aurai pas renoncé: [...] mon respect pour mon homosexualité et celle des autres [...]' (p. 189) ('I shall have died for a cause, faithful to the last: [...] my respect for my homosexuality and that of others [...]', p. 150). In the context of his sexuality, which is the feature that defined him before he became HIV-positive (p. 163),[54] in the middle of the book Dreuilhe comments on his loss of subjectivity, especially after he stopped having an active sex life (it took him a year to settle into abstinence, p. 94). He then endorsed instead and *by default* the subjectivity of a PWA (p. 162). He is now again claiming the subjectivity of being a homosexual with pride and dignity (p. 194). This means he has worked through negative images and has therefore entered a process of reintegration. Dreuilhe sees a trade-off between giving up active sexuality and feeling in harmony between body and soul; the war has now become a *holy* war enabling him to access a mystical life through asceticism (pp. 97–98).

It is no coincidence that Dreuilhe chose to write his book in French, the language of his family, his *mother* tongue, claiming that he could never have written this book in English because an adopted language always betrays one (p. 19) – interestingly enough his psychoanalysis must have been conducted in English. He speaks of France as the country he had left behind now returning towards him, and of French culture and his body being the two pillars to which he clings, saying that he knew from the age of infant stammering that his first and last hope was the French language (pp. 18–19).

In the last sentence of *Corps à corps*, Dreuilhe lucidly prepares for suicide, proving that he is nobody's fool regarding where his illness is leading, despite claiming that it had stopped deteriorating while he was writing his book: 'Quand je serai Berlin [*sic*] en mai 1945, il sera peut-être temps que je nous empoisonne, le SIDA et moi, dans son bunker' (p. 201) ('When I become Berlin in May 1945, it may perhaps be time for me to poison us both, AIDS and me, in its bunker').[55] There are traces of narcissistic omnipotence in the comparison with Hitler. The ambiguity towards AIDS mentioned at the outset of this chapter is still present here. Everyone knows that Hitler poisoned himself with his *lover*, Eva Braun, who had just become his wife (they had been married a few hours beforehand), and Dreuilhe uses 'nous', intimating that AIDS is his lover. *Corps à corps* seems in this instance to be referring to a sexual encounter, or at any rate to the battle between Eros and Thanatos. Earlier, Dreuilhe had evoked the fact that HIV-positive people are walking time-bombs (p. 44), and poisoning them both in a bunker is a way of not incurring any other casualties.

The book was finished on 14 July 1987 (p. 201). While writing in

New York, Dreuilhe shows that his heart is in France since this is France's national festival, commemorating the storming of the Bastille, and also *the beginning of a civil war*. This could be Dreuilhe's last wishful gesture within the framework of a literature of mobilisation. Indeed the history of the AIDS crisis shows 1987 as being a turning point in terms of mobilisation and prevention. On 28 November 1988, the year that his book was published in North America, Alain Emmanuel Dreuilhe died of AIDS-related illnesses in New York.

I claimed right at the outset of this study that Dreuilhe's book could be seen as being part of the broad definition of literature. Its literary quality is emphasised in the back cover text: 'Mais c'est un texte traversé par le plaisir d'écrire, où le ressourcement littéraire devient une arme contre les assauts du mal.' ('But it is a text permeated by the pleasure of writing where newly found literary energy becomes a weapon against the assaults of the disease.') As we saw with Wetsel, the book invited controversy both in America and in France. But this does not necessarily imply that *Corps à corps* was recuperated by the dominant discourse. Here is perhaps the first example of a text, ambiguous as it is at times, not recuperated by the discourse of monogamous heterosexual masculinities and femininities or by the 'just punishment' narrative. For the first time perhaps in the history of AIDS writing in France, 'speaking out' means 'breaking out'.

At the beginning of this chapter, I mentioned Dreuilhe noting one difference between AIDS and war in that PWAs are dying for no reason when in war there is supposed to be a cause worth fighting for. Near the end of the book, he talks about fighting for homosexuality, his beleaguered land (p. 161), and compares his act of writing to lighting a candle in the dark, hoping for others to join in so that it becomes a torchlight parade (p. 123). His book stands as a memorial to this belief.

Conclusion

E arly AIDS writing went on in the margins of literature. Most of the books lack the usual literary qualities and yet found their way to being published and read. They have a fragmented, raw authenticity which makes them worth studying today. One can imagine the pressure of the subject-matter building up throughout the early 1980s and the bubble bursting when these texts were published, at times at the expense of literariness and often in the form of fragmented pieces rather than as fully fledged texts, reflecting the dwindling energy of their authors. They are not all built on the same model, and the subjective positioning of the presumed authors, both in terms of gender and sexual orientation, also varies widely. Dreuilhe and Aron aside, as far as we can tell, none of them had ever appeared in print before. Since these writings mostly come from the margins, it is unreasonable to expect polished elegance from them. In fact, it is *precisely* because most of them were not deemed to be 'literature' that they were allowed to be published: they could not 'contaminate' the literary establishment and by extension the majority of the heterosexual population whose serological status was negative.

My archaeology of AIDS writing has helped to bring to light what had been covered up; these books are mostly out of print and would almost certainly not have been published in the 1990s. Their lack of conformity to usual literary conventions has allowed me to unearth different meanings in these texts that might otherwise have remained obscure: for example, the centrality of the concept of avalanche in Simonin's book, Laygues' ambivalent voyeurism, the unresolved grief in Juliette and Winer, the importance of *phantasy* in Dreuilhe. In almost all cases, the writing process afforded these writers the means to psychic reintegration after an earlier splitting, and a new positioning as social subjects.

In the case of the three AIDS fictions, we saw that they have the style of unpretentious popular narrative and yet are engaged in literary trickery and artifice. They all to some degree make use of AIDS on the way to making some other point or telling some other story; for example, a morality tale with the leitmotiv that PWAs deserve their punishment. The thriller genre adopted by Winer and to a lesser extent by Juliette reflects a specific time in the AIDS pandemic, as analysed by Weeks, that of moral panic. Williamson classifies this type of fiction as follows:

> On the one hand, the HIV virus enters a kind of Noddy-land of narrative meaning, where it takes on particular characteristics, goals and functions – even 'preferences'. On the other, however, it joins the morass of unthinkability in which homosexuality is already (for many people) placed, a Gothic territory where fears are flung out into a sort of mental wasteland beyond the castle walls of the ego.[1]

These narratives evoke terror and/or pity as the only emotions available to deal with AIDS.[2]

My genealogy of AIDS fiction (looking at power and knowledge relations) has been focused principally on the back cover blurbs (usually written by editors). These reveal that the texts were framed as part of the dominant discourse of social and sexual regulation aiming to preserve the dominant form of monogamous heterosexual relationships: 'Particular discourses set parameters through which desire is produced, regulated and channelled'.³ Fiction was always more likely to be recuperated by the dominant discourse, and this could explain why the gay men studied in this book chose the testimonial-type of writing. Heterosexuality needed to be the ruling framework, as in the books by Juliette, Laygues and Winer. Through attempts to reaffirm norms of gender and heterosexual masculinities and femininities at some point of maximum vulnerability and openness to deconstruction following the sexual liberation of the 1970s and early 1980s, the French state showed that its constructions of nationality/sexuality relationships were felt to be under threat. Assumptions about heterosexual relations can be situated historically and imply the workings of power-knowledge relations. Behind this particular discourse are Christian ideals associated with monogamous relationships and family life. Another study could well uncover the influence of Catholicism on early AIDS writing in France.⁴ One of the main characteristics of this corpus is the virulence with which vindictive judgmental narratives are visited on PWAs, notably with the theme of 'just punishment'.

There is no more extreme example of this than the first book to be published on the subject in 1985. The back cover blurb of *Sida, Témoignage sur la vie et la mort de Martin* describes sexuality as a dangerous business. The object of the book is not to demystify AIDS (as the start of the text would have us believe) but to warn us that if we follow adventurous desire, we will meet an unhappy end. The same claim is made in the book: reflecting on Martin's life one year after his death, Hélène (the first-person narrator) writes, making inferences from what he said at different times, that she is *certain* Martin saw his illness as a price he had to pay for his life of pleasure, when there is not a shred of evidence to validate her statement. This statement is very similar to the right-wing religious ideology that claimed that AIDS was a punishment from God for homosexuality. The back cover text of *Pourquoi moi?* claims that the prevalence of AIDS puts sexual freedom in jeopardy; the implication is that if you are an 'unattached, young and ambitious female journalist', there is some logic in your contracting AIDS. What is also implied is that men must be wary of women like Juliette, and therefore of casual sex, for they could become infected. 'Death for a few minutes of pleasure' is the message of the back cover of *Bienvenue dans le monde du Sida!*, equating sex and death; this is a very puritanical and repressive statement in the context of the crisis of 1988. Implicit in the text is the assumption that monogamous heterosexual sexuality is the only way to be and remain safe from the 'killer' virus. These three examples show the problems associated with writing about a new and taboo topic, and the way that the ruling modes of sexualities are produced/ reproduced in such writing. The most effective border patrol in the first two works is the back cover text which polices 'forbidden' desires. This is reinforced by the confessional mode, especially with Juliette's text. This is a familiar means through which power is exercised, as demonstrated by Foucault in *The History of Sexuality*[5] where the practice of confession is described as defining, constituting and regulating sexuality.[6]

By giving such prominence to the back cover blurb of these texts, I am aware that I could give the impression of setting up an opposition in which an author with supposed *integrity* has his or her good intentions sabotaged by the editing and publishing process. However, we have seen that there is no such opposition, and that the authors themselves (i.e., the texts themselves) are responsible for their own attitudes and prejudices towards homosexuality and PWAs.

Throughout, women are represented either as witches and even killers (Juliette, Mona Hessler in Winer), often because they take an active part in defining their sexuality, or as self-sacrificing Madonnas (Hélène Laygues, Dreuilhe's wife Kristine and Winer's fiancée Karine Wooley).[7] This latter representation is rooted in Catholicism: 'Within Catholicism there are subject positions which validate and even celebrate particular modes of femininity, for instance, an approach to traditional family life [...] in the case of female sexuality, for example, sex is defined as naturally heterosexual and procreative and femininity is implicitly masochistic'.[8] This is almost an exact portrait of Hélène Laygues, although as we saw she is anything but powerless.

The second part of my book dealt with AIDS testimonies all written by gay men; they also all made at least one television appearance to talk about being a PWA. I have shown the 'political' project which most of these texts are engaged in. For instance, Dreuilhe's book is part of the literature of mobilisation crucial to the mid-1980s, when there was general apathy among governments who believed that AIDS was mostly affecting the gay community. Simonin fought to be published and heard, knowing that silence equalled death. Aron was aware of the risks of being misunderstood when he agreed to speak in an interview about *his* AIDS. The tragedy of both 'Mon sida' and the television programme about Aron is that this site of personal and political change was overlooked not only by the dominant discourse but also by some PWAs and homosexuals; 'speaking out' is not necessarily 'breaking out'.

AIDS testimony is struggling to find an appropriate means to present something previously unknown that is being ignored or misrepresented. One of the main difficulties is that there are only conventional means available for presenting something that is understood *not to be amenable* to conventional representations. This problem is evident in Simonin, whose book does not specify any genre on the cover, and in Aron's interview and television programme. Neither of them can escape the 'just punishment' narrative, as was seen in the way 'aveu' was constructed as 'confession' for Aron. However, this does not detract from the fact that Aron's intervention marks a real watershed in the history of intellectuals speaking and writing about being HIV-positive. As exemplified by the testimony of the television programme's assistant-director, once one has spoken, others will follow. Dreuilhe invented the genre of the 'diary-tract' in order to move from the individual experience to the collective one, from his own to general mobilisation. He also managed to avoid the 'just punishment' narrative, even though we saw that his book was criticised on both sides of the Atlantic. As I suggested at the beginning of Chapter 4, testimonial writing is not only personally therapeutic but also an attempt to diagnose the social pathologies that are responsible for the embattlement of AIDS subjects, pathologies which are so embedded in society that they are not recognised as pathologies. The probability that these testimonies would fail to be heard was high precisely because of society's

146

deafness and blindness to its own illness. Testifying to the difficulties of witnessing as both Simonin and Aron do is itself an act of testimony, a victory against the hegemonic order.[9]

I made the point in the introduction that the writers under study here are the antecedents of another group of AIDS writers (Bourdin, Collard, De Duve, Guibert etc.) who were successful in the 1990s. Hence what my archaeology has unearthed is that there is a prehistory as well as a history of AIDS writing. It is beyond the scope of this book to *prove* that these texts paved the way for the success of AIDS writing in the 1990s (one would have to do a comparative study of the two groups, of the reception of the texts and of their readership etc.). Most of the 1990s writings were thinly disguised, fictionalised autobiographies. What these writers may have learned from the experience of the writers considered here are the distancing techniques necessary to 'contain' the public's fears. This allowed readers to invest themselves emotionally in the narratives, a process which was immensely helped by the shifting attitude of the general public towards PWAs in the early 1990s. Perhaps the raw authenticity of testimonial writing contributed to the general public holding back in the mid-1980s. As I mentioned in the introduction, Hervé Guibert's first book about AIDS, *À l'ami qui ne m'a pas sauvé la vie*, published in 1990, which begins 'I have had AIDS for three months', is an example of what I call a *'roman faux'*, a novel in which *'I tell lies'*. Hence Guibert had learned from the pioneers in the field to stay clear of traditional novels, testimonial writing or autobiographies, or at least to fictionalise the autobiography (the act of writing is a fictionalisation *per se*, but there are different *degrees* of 'fictionalising' a text) in deciding to write about AIDS.

But as Chambers believes, the success of the 1990s writers may have been purchased at the price of a certain complicity with cultural expectations, including expectations about *high* cultural writing. This in turn devalues further what we could call *low* cultural writing, as in the case of Simonin's book. Certainly some personal narratives of the 1990s show few collective concerns, as ACT-UP critically noted. So, in their very failure, non-literary writers such as Simonin or Aron might have been more exemplary witnesses than the much more successful literary generation that followed.

What were the different writing/literary options on offer to these mostly first-time authors who wanted to write about AIDS? If we take the specific example of Simonin, how else could he have been heard? I have argued that *Danger de vie* is important because of its very flaws and through its significant silences. In the case of Dreuilhe, he had to invent a language outside of conventional psychoanalysis, in order to survive psychically and to *phantasise* that the day of the allies' landing was approaching in order to counter the general apathy he sensed around the AIDS crisis. There is no clear distinction between AIDS fiction and testimony, but rather some blurred boundaries. Whether they belong to one category or the other, all the books considered here reflect the sense of isolation and the lack of community support, specific to France's reaction to the AIDS crisis.[10] For instance, Simonin has to project himself into a collective grief (the avalanche) in order to feel legitimated and supported in his own feelings of loss and devastation: this is the epitome of the fate of a gay PWA in France in the mid-1980s.

In Holocaust testimonial, what is important is not the books that have been published by survivors, but the stories never told of the people who perished in the gas chambers. There is a partial parallel at work here with early AIDS writing,[11] though I am not comparing the two and would resist such comparisons. Most of the books considered here are out of print and therefore buried. With the possible exception of Dreuilhe's book (and even here the appeal for mobilisation against the illness would have to reflect the evolving situation of a PWA, especially in the West, during the new millennium), most of these texts would not be published today.[12] My excavation work has unearthed these stories and my genealogical work has shown the various power/ knowledge relations that shaped them, unmasking yet again how the governing position operates and how it perpetuates its ruling framework over subordinated others. In Chapter 5, I mentioned Dreuilhe comparing his act of writing to lighting a candle in the dark, hoping for others to join in so that it becomes a torchlight parade.[13] I hope that this book might reignite these flames so that, together, their glowing testimony should stand as a memorial to early AIDS writing in France. This memorial records the wide range of writing strategies, from disruptive to conservative, as well as the 'political' project which most of these texts were engaged in. It also records the discriminations that PWAs endured in the 1980s, and the scandalous lack of early prevention in France which cost the lives of thousands of people, mostly gay men. This is why these *HIV Stories* should not be forgotten.

Notes

Introduction

1 Hélène Laygues, *Sida, Témoignage sur la vie et la mort de Martin*, Paris, Hachette, 1985; Michel Simonin, *Danger de vie*, Paris, Librairie Séguier, 1986; Jean-Paul Aron, 'Mon sida', interview in *Le Nouvel Observateur*, 30 October-5 November 1987, by Elisabeth Schemla; revised by J.-P Aron and published by Christian Bourgois Editeur, *Mon sida*, 1988; Aron, television programme on Antenne 2, 21 June 1988, 'Sida: après l'aveu' ('AIDS: after the confession'); Juliette, *Pourquoi moi? Confession d'une jeune femme d'aujourd'hui*, Paris, Robert Laffont, 1987; Alain Emmanuel Dreuilhe, *Corps à Corps, Journal de Sida*, Paris, Gallimard, 1987 (translated into English as *Mortal Embrace: Living with AIDS*, trans. Linda Coverdale, New York, Hill and Wang, 1988); Mike Winer, *Bienvenue dans le monde du sida!*, Monaco, Le Rocher, 1988.

I have chosen not to include the following declared *novels* all published between 1985 and 1988 which are generally recognised to be partly/wholly about AIDS: Valéry Luria (pseudonym for pianist Valéry Afanassiev), *La Chute de Babylone*, Paris, Belfont, 1985; Guy Hocquenghem, *Ève*, Paris, Albin Michel 1987; Dominique Fernandez, *La Gloire du paria*, Paris, Grasset, 1987; Yves de Mellis, *Un Mal qui répand la Terreur*, Paris, Barré et Dayez, 1988; Gabriel Matzneff, *Harrison Plaza*, Paris, La Table Ronde, 1988.

2 One notable exception being the article by Hélène Jaccomard 'Du sexisme dans les écrits du sida', *French Cultural Studies*, Vol. 9, Part 3, No. 27, October 1998, pp. 321–35.

150

3   Ross Chambers, *Facing It, AIDS Diaries and the Death of the Author*, Ann Arbor, MI, University of Michigan Press, 1998, p. 18.

4   Timothy F. Murphy, 'Testimony', in Timothy F. Murphy and Suzanne Poirier, eds, *Writing AIDS: Gay Literature, Language and Analysis*, New York, Columbia University Press, 1993, pp. 306–20 (p. 307).

5   I shall use the terms 'homosexual' and 'gay' according to the context, although I am aware that in the Anglo-Saxon world each term carries a certain political significance, unlike in France in the late 1980s.

6   Michel Danthe, 'Le sida et les lettres: un bilan francophone', *Équinoxe*, No. 5, Spring 1991, pp. 51–85 (p. 52).

7   Roland Barthes, *Image, Music, Text*, New York, Hill and Wang, 1977, p. 145.

8   Foucault talks about an 'author' being an extrapolation from a reading practice, the result of 'projections, in terms always more or less psychological, of our way of handling texts'. Michel Foucault, *Language, Counter-Memory, Practice*, Ithaca, NY, Cornell University Press, 1977, p. 127; Barthes, *Image, Music, Text*, pp. 142–43.

9   Julian Henriques, Wendy Hollway, Cathy Urwin, Couze Venn and Valerie Walkerdine, *Changing the Subject: Psychology, social regulation and subjectivity*, London, Methuen, 1984, p. 114.

10 Chambers, *Facing It*, p. 16. For a study of genre, see Jacques Derrida, 'The Law of Genre', in Derek Attridge, ed., *Acts of Literature*, London, Routledge, 1992, pp. 221–52. Also Anne Freadman and Amanda Macdonald, *What is this thing called 'genre'?*, Mount Nebo, Queensland, Boombana Publications, 1992.

11 Mark Freeman, *Rewriting the Self: History, Memory, Narrative*, London, Routledge, 1993, p. 8.

12 Chambers, *Facing It*, p. viii.

13 Chambers, *Facing It*, p. 22.

14 Guibert's book seems to eclipse what went on before 1990. Hence Emily Apter talks about Guibert as 'France's premier *sida* novelist': Emily Apter, 'Fantom Images: Hervé Guibert and the Writing of "sida" in France', in Murphy and Poirier, eds, *Writing AIDS*, pp. 83–97 (p. 83).

15 Cyril Collard, *Les Nuits fauves*, Paris, Flammarion, 1989. This film, which Collard wrote, directed and in which he had the main male lead role, came out in 1992 and in the English-speaking world under the title *Savage Nights*.

16 Hugo Marsan, 'Le roman du sida', *Gai Pied Hebdo*, No. 451, 3 January 1991, p. 20.

17 I argue in *Hervé Guibert: Voices of the Self*, Liverpool, Liverpool University Press, 1999, that Guibert's first book about AIDS (*À l'ami qui ne m'a pas sauvé la vie*), which starts with 'I have had AIDS for three months', is an example of what I call a *roman faux*, a novel in which '*I tell lies*'. Hence Guibert would have learned from the pioneers in the field to stay clear of traditional novels, testimonial writing or autobiographies, in deciding to write about AIDS.

18 Marsan, 'Le roman du sida'.

19 Joseph Lévy and Alexis Nouss, *Sida-Fiction, Essai d'anthropologie romanesque*, Lyon, Presses universitaires de Lyon, 1994.

20 Jean-Luc Maxence, *Les Écrivains sacrifiés des années Sida*, Paris, Bayard Éditions, 1995.

21 Danthe, 'Le sida et les lettres'; François Boullant, 'Latex, mensonges et melo ... Sida et littérature', *Actes*, Nos. 71–72, 1990, pp. 50–58; David Wetsel, 'The Best of Times, the Worst of Times: The Emerging Literature of AIDS in France', in Emmanuel S. Nelson, ed., *AIDS: The Literary Response*, New York, Twayne Publishers, 1992, pp. 95–113; Joseph Lévy and Alexis Nouss, 'La violence dans la fiction romanesque sur le Sida', *Bulletin de Thanatologie*, No. 95–96, November 1993, pp. 115–44; Lévy and Nouss, *Sida-Fiction*; Maxence, *Les Écrivains sacrifiés des années Sida*.

22 One notable exception is the effort by Didier Éribon to introduce gay and lesbian studies in France: *Les Études gay et lesbiennes*, Paris, Centre Georges Pompidou, 1998.

23 Henriques et al., *Changing the Subject*, p. 118.

24 I am not at all in agreement with James Morrison's thesis, which sees post-structuralism as operating in the sphere of allegory regarding AIDS (in part yes but not exclusively) and stigmatising those who have the illness. I believe that at the root of post-structuralism is a political project. James Morrison, 'The Repression of the Returned: AIDS and Allegory', in Nelson, ed., *AIDS: The Literary Response*, pp. 167–74.

25 Jeff Hearn, *The Gender of Oppression*, Brighton, Wheatsheaf Books, 1987, p. 91.

26 Arthur Brittan, *Masculinity and Power*, Oxford, Blackwell, 1989, pp. 168–69.

27 Michael S. Kimmel and Martin P. Levine, 'Men and *AIDS*', in Franklin Abbott, ed., *Men and Intimacy*, San Francisco, The Crossing Press Freedom, 1990, pp. 90–102 (p. 99).

28 See R. Harvey 'Sidaïques/sidéens: French Discourses on AIDS', *Contemporary French Civilization*, Vol. 16, No. 192, Summer/Fall 1992, pp. 308–35.

29 Jeffrey Weeks, *Sexuality and its Discontents*, London, Routledge, 1985, p. 47.

30 Weeks, *Sexuality and its Discontents*.

31 Jeffrey Weeks, *Sex, Politics and Society*, Harlow, Longman, 2nd edn, 1994, p. 301.

32 Wetsel, 'The Best of Times, the Worst of Times', p. 95.

33 Wetsel, 'The Best of Times, the Worst of Times', p. 95.

34 ACT-UP Paris, *Le Sida, Combien de divisions?*, Paris, Dagorno, 1994, p. 369. See also pp. 314–16, 367–68.

35 ACT-UP Paris, *Le Sida*, p. 316.

36 Hugo Marsan, *La Vie blessée*, Paris, Maren Sell, 1989, p. 71.

37 Marsan, *La Vie blessée*, p. 139.

38 ACT-UP Paris, *Le Sida*, p. 314.

39 James Agar, 'Writing the "Histoire" of AIDS in France', *French Cultural Studies*, Vol. 9, Part 3, No. 27, October 1998, p. 415.

40 In Frédéric Martel, *The Pink and the Black: Homosexuals in France since 1968*, trans. Jane Marie Todd, Stanford, CA, Stanford University Press, 2000, pp. 367–72. Original edition: *Le Rose et le noir, Les homosexuels en France depuis 1968*, Paris, Seuil, 1996.

41 Marsan, *La Vie blessée*, pp. 60, 101, 103–04.

42 Martel, *The Pink and the Black*, p. 422, note 38.

43 David Caron, '*Liberté, Égalité, Séropositivité:* AIDS, the French Republic, and the Question of Community', *French Cultural Studies*, Vol. 9, Part 3, No. 27, October 1998, p. 283.

44 Caron, '*Liberté, Égalité, Séropositivité*'. In the introduction to his book, *AIDS in French Culture: Social Ills, Literary Cures*, Madison, WI, University of Wisconsin Press, 2001, Caron shows how the late nineteenth-century construction of male homosexuality has provided the conceptual and rhetorical frameworks within which AIDS discourses and counter-discourses were produced and disseminated in contemporary French culture, notably with the concept of 'dégénérescence' ('degeneracy') at the root of homophobia.

45 Caron, '*Liberté, Égalité, Séropositivité*', p. 284.

46 Caron, '*Liberté, Égalité, Séropositivité*', p. 285.

47 Caron, '*Liberté, Égalité, Séropositivité*', p. 292.

48 Alec Hargreaves, *Immigration, 'Race' and Ethnicity in Contemporary France*, London, Routledge, 1995, pp. 189–97.

49 Murray Pratt, 'The defence of the straight state: heteronormativity, AIDS in France, and the space of the nation', *French Cultural Studies*, Vol. 9, Part 3, No. 27, October 1998, p. 267.

50 Bernard Paillard, *L'Épidémie: carnets d'un sociologue*, Paris, Stock, 1994, p. 31.

51 Larys Frogier, 'Homosexuals, and the AIDS Crisis in France', in Joshua Oppenheimer and Helena Reckitt, eds, *Acting on AIDS: Sex, Drugs and Politics*, London, Serpent's Tail, 1997, p. 353 and p. 359, note 17.

52 The point is made by both Frank Arnal, *Résister ou disparaître: les homosexuels face au sida: la prévention de 1982 à 1992*, Paris, L'Harmattan, 1993, p. 73, and Jean de Savigny, *Le SIDA et les fragilités françaises: nos réactions face à l'épidémie*, Paris, Albin Michel, 1995, p. 57. See also Murray Pratt, 'AIDS Prevention, Gay Identity and National Homophobia in France', in Joe Andrew, Malcolm Crook, Diana Holmes and Eva Kolinsky, eds, *Why Europe? Problems of Culture and Identity*, London, Macmillan, 2000, pp. 142–69.

53 Pratt, 'The defence of the straight state', p. 271.

54 Pratt, 'The defence of the straight state', p. 265.

55 Arnal, *Résister ou disparaître*, p. 103 and p. 59.

56 Hervé Guibert, *À l'ami qui ne m'a pas sauvé la vie*, Paris, Gallimard, 1990, p. 21.

57 Frogier, 'Homosexuals, and the AIDS crisis in France', p. 349.

58 Frogier, 'Homosexuals, and the AIDS crisis in France', p. 356.

59 Gregory Woods, 'La fin d'Arcadie: *Gai Pied* and the "cancer gai"', *French Cultural Studies*, Vol. 9, Part 3, No. 27, October 1998, p. 297.

60 Cited in Pratt, 'The defence of the straight state', p. 272.

61 Martel, *The Pink and the Black*, p. 136.

62 Martel, *The Pink and the Black*, pp. 144 and 152.

63 For an excellent monograph, see Bill Marshall, *Guy Hocquenghem: Theorising the Gay Nation*, London, Pluto Press, 1996.

64 Martel, *The Pink and the Black*, p. 153.
65 Martel, *The Pink and the Black*, p. 178.
66 Martel, *The Pink and the Black*, p. 193.
67 Simon Watney, *Practices of Freedom: Selected Writings on HIV/AIDS*, London, River Oram Press, 1994, p. 246.
68 Martel, *The Pink and the Black*, p. 200.
69 For a study of a comparison between France, the United Kingdom and Sweden in their response to the AIDS crisis, see Michel Setbon, *Pouvoirs contre sida*, Paris, Seuil, 1993.
70 Woods, 'La fin d'Arcadie', p. 301.
71 Woods, 'La fin d'Arcadie', p. 305.
72 Martel, *The Pink and the Black*, pp. 208–09.
73 Pratt, 'The defence of the straight state', p. 271.
74 Technically, it was Patrick Meyer in 1983 who founded the first association: 'Vaincre le sida' ('Conquering AIDS').
75 For more details, see Martel, *The Pink and the Black*, p. 221.
76 Frogier, 'Homosexuals, and the AIDS crisis in France', p. 356.
77 Martel, *The Pink and the Black*, p. 236.
78 Martel, *The Pink and the Black*, p. 240.
79 Martel, *The Pink and the Black*, pp. 332 and 418, note 18. Watney makes the judicious point that if one compares the French government's response to the troubles in Corsica, which affect barely 200,000 French citizens, with their response to the needs of French homosexuals, one becomes aware of the scale of French homophobia by omission. Watney, *Practices of Freedom*, pp. 247–48.
80 Louis Pauwels, 'Le monôme des zombies', *Figaro Magazine*, 6 December 1986.
81 Martel, *The Pink and the Black*, p. 252.
82 Martel, *The Pink and the Black*, pp. 248–49.
83 Jean-Baptiste Brunet, 'Tirer sérieusement des leçons', interview by J. C. Cauchy and J. Y. Le Talec, *Gai Pied Hebdo*, 24 October 1991.
84 Lee Edelman, *Homographesis*, London, Routledge, 1994, p. 96.
85 Edelman, *Homographesis*.
86 Edelman, *Homographesis*.
87 Edelman, *Homographesis*.
88 Edelman, *Homographesis*, p. 94.
89 Lawrence R. Schehr, 'Hervé Guibert under Bureaucratic Quarantine', *L'Esprit créateur*, Vol. XXXIV, No. 1, Spring 1994, pp. 73–82 (pp. 76–77).
90 Judith Laurence Pastore, 'Suburban AIDS: Alice Hoffman's *At Risk*', in Nelson, ed., *AIDS: The Literary Response*, p. 41. See also Judith Laurence Pastore, ed., *Confronting AIDS through Literature*, Chicago, University of Illinois Press, 1993.
91 Joseph Dewey, 'Music for a Closing: Responses to AIDS in Three American Novels', in Nelson, ed., *AIDS: The Literary Response*, pp. 23–38 (38).
92 Diana Fuss, 'Inside Out', in Diana Fuss, ed., *Inside/Out: Lesbian Theories, Gay Theories*, New York, Routledge, 1991, pp. 1–10 (p. 5).
93 Birger Angvik, 'Textual Constellations: AIDS and the Love of Writing in the

Postmodern Era', *Journal of Latin American Cultural Studies*, Vol. 7, No. 2, 1998, pp. 165–83 (p. 169). This relatively recent article deals at length with this question.

94 Jonathan Dollimore, *Sexual Dissidence. Augustine to Wilde, Freud to Foucault*, Oxford, Clarendon Press, 1991, quoted in Angvik, 'Textual Constellations', p. 169.

95 Chris Weedon, *Feminist Practice and Poststructuralist Theory*, Oxford, Blackwell, 1987, p. 169.

96 Lee Edelman 'The Plague of Discourse: Politics, Literary Theory, and AIDS', *South Atlantic Quarterly*, Vol. 88, No. 1, Winter 1989, p. 316, note 1.

97 Chambers, *Facing It*, p. 22.

98 Chambers, *Facing It*, pp. 23, 128. See also Murphy, 'Testimony', pp. 306–20.

99 I would like to salute in passing the contributors to the special issue of *French Cultural Studies* on 'Personal Voices, Personal Experiences', edited by Brian Rigby, Vol. 10, Part 3, No. 30, October 1999, which gave me some sense of companionship for my own experience of writing myself into the picture.

100 'Hervé Guibert ou la radicalisation du projet sartrien d'écriture existentielle', in Ralph Sarkonak, ed., *Le Corps textuel d'Hervé Guibert*, Paris, Minard, 1997, pp. 25–42.

101 Marsan, *La Vie blessée*, p. 13.

102 Caron, *AIDS in French Culture*; Larry Kramer, *The Normal Heart*, New York, Plume, 1985.

103 Cited in Valerie Walkerdine, 'Video replay: families, films and fantasy', in her *Schoolgirl Fictions*, London, Verso, 1990, p. xi.

104 Freeman, *Rewriting the Self*, p. 81.

105 Walkerdine, *Schoolgirl Fictions*, p. 202, note 2.

106 This distinction was first suggested by Ross Chambers.

107 Danthe, 'Le sida et les lettres', p. 52.

108 Edelman, 'The Plague of Discourse', p. 315.

1 Laygues: The Ambiguity in Witnessing

1 Hélène Laygues, *Sida, Témoignage sur la vie et la mort de Martin*, Paris, Hachette, 1985. All references to this book are inserted in brackets in the body of the text.

2 Ross Chambers, 'AIDS and the Culture of Accompaniment in France', *French Cultural Studies*, Vol. 9, Part 3, No. 27, October 1998, pp. 399–409. See also Murphy, 'Testimony', pp. 306–20.

3 Danthe, 'Le sida et les lettres', p. 52. Juliette and Mike Winer are also pseudonyms.

4 Judith Butler, *Gender Trouble: Feminism and the Subversion of Identity*, New York, Routledge, 1990.

5 Woods, 'La fin d'Arcadie', p. 297.

6 See Pratt, 'The defence of the straight state', pp. 269–71; Wetsel, 'The Best of Times, the Worst of Times', pp. 95–96.

7 This is typical of the French response throughout the early to mid-1980s of

seeing AIDS as an American phenomenon. According to Wetsel, 'French AIDS literature is riddled with passages in which characters attempt to trace the source of their infection to someone who visited New York or San Francisco in the early 1980s.' Wetsel, 'The Best of Times, the Worst of Times', p. 96.

8 R.W. Connell, *Masculinities*, Oxford, Polity Press, 1995, pp. 161–62.

9 Woods, 'La fin d'Arcadie'.

10 Woods, 'La fin d'Arcadie', p. 296.

11 Anna Marie Smith, *New Right Discourse on Race and Sexuality: Britain 1968–1990*, Cambridge, Cambridge University Press, 1994, p. 102.

12 I should at this point declare my own personal involvement in this story, to complement the general points I made in the introduction. I became aware of this involvement when a friend told me that my reading was relentless. By this I took him to mean that I was overtly preoccupied with 'denouncing' the character of Hélène. Inevitably, I am the male reader gazing at the representation of a female narrative voice and I have the power/knowledge to construct her in a certain way, and to objectify her; I become the voyeur of Hélène and the production of desire is inextricably intertwined in these textual exchanges.

13 Michel Foucault, *History of Sexuality, Vol. 1, The Will to Knowledge*, Harmondsworth, Penguin, 1981, p. 101.

14 D. L. Steinberg, D. Epstein and R. Johnson, eds, *Border Patrols*, London, Cassell, 1997.

15 Peter Redman, 'Invasion of the Monstrous Others: Heterosexual Masculinities, the "AIDS Carrier" and the Horror Genre', in Steinberg et al., eds, *Border Patrols*, pp. 98–116.

16 P. Stallybrass and A. White, *The Politics and Poetics of Transgression*, London, Methuen, 1986.

17 Redman, 'Invasion of the Monstrous Others', p. 109.

18 Butler, *Gender Trouble*.

19 Judith Butler, 'Melancholy Gender/Refused Identification', in Maurice Berger, Brian Wallis and Simon Watson, eds, *Constructing Masculinity*, London, Routledge, 1995, p. 31.

20 Butler, 'Melancholy Gender/Refused Identification'.

21 Simon Watney, *Policing Desire. Pornography, AIDS and the Media*, London, Methuen, 1987, p. 12.

22 Redman, 'Invasion of the Monstrous Others', p. 111.

23 Indeed, this is the fate of desire, since according to feminist poststructuralists, in line with Lacan, 'Desire is a product of language and is subject to the constant deferral of satisfaction equivalent to the constant deferral of meaning in language'; Weedon, *Feminist Practice and Poststructuralist Theory*, p. 51.

24 See in particular Walkerdine, *Schoolgirl Fictions*.

25 Juliet Mitchell, ed., *The Selected Melanie Klein*, Harmondsworth, Penguin, 1991.

26 Judith Williamson, 'Every Virus Tells a Story. The Meanings of HIV and AIDS', in Erica Carter and Simon Watney, eds, *Taking Liberties, AIDS and Cultural Politics*, London, Serpent's Tail, 1989, p. 80.

27 Chambers, 'AIDS and the Culture of Accompaniment', p. 400.

28 Chambers, *Facing It*, pp. 82–83.

29 Weedon, *Feminist Practice and Poststructuralist Theory*, p. 83.

30 For an interesting article on the subject, see Leo Bersani, 'Is the Rectum a Grave?', in Douglas Crimp, ed., *AIDS: Cultural Analysis, Cultural Activism*, Cambridge, MA, MIT Press, 1988, pp. 197–222. A different viewpoint is offered by Guy Hocquenghem, *Le Désir homosexuel*, Paris, Éditions universitaires, 1972.

31 As we will see in Chapter 2, on being diagnosed, Juliette also constructs herself as diabolical. The influence of Catholicism is very powerful.

32 Weedon, *Feminist Practice and Poststructuralist Theory*, p. 96.

2 Juliette: Masculinist Desires and Sexualities

1 Juliette, *Pourquoi moi?*, Paris, Robert Laffont, 1987. All references to this book are inserted in brackets in the body of the text.

2 'Un historien face à la littérature du sida', avec le professeur Mirko Grmek, *Équinoxe*, No. 5, Spring 1991, p. 37.

3 Freeman, *Rewriting the Self*, p. 81.

4 C. Coria, *El Sexo Oculto del Dinero*, Buenos Aires, Grupo Editor Latino-americano, Coleccion Controversia, 1986, p. 23.

5 Lynne Segal, *Slow Motion: Changing Masculinities, Changing Men*, London, Virago, 1990, p. 212.

6 Segal, *Slow Motion*, p. 215.

7 Segal, *Slow Motion*, p. 215.

8 Jessica Benjamin, *The Bonds of Love: Psychoanalysis, feminism and the problem of domination*, London, Virago, 1990, especially pp. 68–74, 'Destruction and survival'.

9 Benjamin, *The Bonds of Love*, p. 87.

10 Benjamin, *The Bonds of Love*, p. 123.

11 Benjamin, *The Bonds of Love*, p. 109.

12 Henriques et al., *Changing the Subject*, p. 222.

13 Pierre Bourdieu, *La Domination masculine*, Paris, Seuil, 1998, p. 87.

14 Bourdieu, *La Domination masculine*.

15 Benjamin, *The Bonds of Love*, p. 89.

16 Benjamin, *The Bonds of Love*, pp. 91ff.

17 Estela V. Welldon, *Mother, Madonna, Whore*, New York, The Guilford Press, 1988. Page references to this volume are inserted in the text in brackets.

18 Welldon, *Mother, Madonna, Whore*, p. iv 'Foreword' by Juliet Mitchell. It should be noted that Welldon's book received mixed reviews, especially as it deals with mothers committing incest and harming their children in other ways. Entering this debate is clearly not the scope of this chapter.

19 Again we come across the issue of the veridicality of this particular episode. All I can say is that Juliette the author, by writing it in the story, makes the narrator, Juliette, occupy a subject-position from which I think it is legitimate for me to

draw out the particular discourses and practices which combine to produce her subjectivity.

20 Benjamin, *The Bonds of Love*, p. 110.

21 Benjamin, *The Bonds of Love*, p. 68.

22 I do not subscribe to the exclusively heterosexual model of a couple. 'Father-figure' can be substituted for 'father', and also same-sex couples acting as parents.

23 J. Krout Tabin, *On the Way to Self*, New York, Columbia University Press, 1985, p. 92.

24 ACT-UP Paris, *Le Sida*, pp. 237–46.

25 See Woods, 'La fin d'Arcadie', pp. 295–305.

26 ACT-UP Paris, *Le Sida*, p. 368.

27 Anne Souyris, 'L'épidémie au féminin', *Le Journal du sida*, No. 48, March 1993, 'Dossier Femmes', pp. 13–14 (p. 14).

28 For a study of AIDS writing and suicide, see Ross Chambers, 'The suicide experiment: Hervé Guibert's AIDS video, *La Pudeur ou l'impudeur*', *L'Esprit créateur*, Vol. XXXVII, No. 3, Fall 1997, pp. 72–82.

29 Annette Thomé-Renault, *Le Traumatisme de la mort annoncée, Psychosomatique et Sida*, Paris, Dunod, 1995, pp. 68–69.

30 Jaccomard, 'Du sexisme dans les écrits du sida', p. 333.

31 Guibert provided a media-friendly angelic face which created a complicated network of desires with the public. See Jean-Pierre Boulé, 'Tout ange est terrible (À propos des articles nécrologiques sur Hervé Guibert)', *L'Esprit créateur*, Vol. XXXVII, No. 3, Fall 1997, pp. 61–71.

32 ACT-UP Paris, *Le Sida*, pp. 174–75.

33 Klaus Theweleit, *Male Fantasies*, Cambridge, Polity Press, 1987, especially pp. 70–75.

34 Theweleit, *Male Fantasies*, pp. 74–75.

35 Weedon, *Feminist Practice and Poststructuralist Theory*, pp. 119–20.

36 Weedon, *Feminist Practice and Poststructuralist Theory*, p. 120.

37 Weedon, *Feminist Practice and Poststructuralist Theory*, p. 120.

38 Henriques et al., *Changing the Subject*, p. 220.

3 Winer: Masculinity, Grief and Sexuality

1 Mike Winer, *Bienvenue dans le monde du sida!*, Monaco, Le Rocher, 1998. References to this book are inserted in brackets in the body of the text.

2 Various expressions seem to indicate that the book was indeed translated from English. For instance, throughout, there are expressions such as 'Rigole pas, tu veux!' (p. 43), and 'Mets-la en veilleuse, tu veux?' (p. 45), respectively 'Don't laugh at me, will you!', and 'Keep your voice down, will you?' which would be ineloquent in French.

3 Chambers, *Facing It*, p. 7.

4 Chambers, *Facing It*, p. 2.

5 Mirko Grmek believes that the root of the story may be factual but that it is significantly distorted by the writing; 'Un historien face à la littérature du sida', p. 37.

6 Danthe, 'Le sida et les lettres', p. 52.

7 Williamson, 'Every Virus Tells a Story', p. 71.

8 Williamson, 'Every Virus Tells a Story', p. 71.

9 Jaccomard, 'Du sexisme dans les écrits du sida', p. 333.

10 ACT-UP Paris, *Le Sida*, pp. 174–75.

11 Marsan, *La Vie blessée*, pp. 139–40.

12 Theweleit, *Male Fantasies*, especially pp. 70–75.

13 Marsan, *La Vie blessée*, p. 74. ACT-UP famously denounced the then president of the United States, Ronald Reagan, who took until 31 May 1987 to pronounce the word 'AIDS', let alone try and do something about it.

14 As late as in 1993, Arnaud Marty-Lavauzelle, chair of the French National AIDS association, wrote that to learn that one is HIV-positive is really the announcement of a death foretold; 'Chronique d'une mort annoncée', *Bulletin de Thanatologie*, No. 95–96, November 1993, p. 71.

15 Henriques et al., *Changing the Subject*, p. 114.

16 Of course, the proviso is that this is Mike Winer's life *as narrated in the text*, the only life of Mike Winer that I am ever likely to know. And my critical intervention could indeed be constructed as another fiction since the narrative is a set of signifying systems that, as reader, I interact with and invest with multiple meanings.

17 Carol Staudacher, *Men and Grief*, San Francisco, New Harbinger Publications, 1991.

18 Staudacher, *Men and Grief*, p. 37.

19 Staudacher, *Men and Grief*, p. 38.

20 Staudacher, *Men and Grief*, p. 39.

21 Mitchell, ed., *The Selected Melanie Klein*, pp. 146–74.

22 Mitchell, ed., *The Selected Melanie Klein*, p. 172.

23 Kimmel and Levine, 'Men and *AIDS*', p. 98.

24 Following Kimmel and Levine, I include both gay and straight men when I talk about heterosexual masculinity.

25 Staudacher, *Men and Grief*, p. 39.

26 Mitchell, ed., *The Selected Melanie Klein*, p. 172.

27 Staudacher, *Men and Grief*, p. 69.

28 My reading is a response to the first-person narratives; it is a reading of the subjectivities 'expressed' in the texts. While this works very well, especially with the AIDS testimony, it is more difficult at times with the AIDS fiction to disentangle personal subjectivities from the social myths that the first-person narrators embody – probably more difficult than my reading would have us believe. This is the case with Hélène, to a lesser extent with Juliette, and most acutely with Mike Winer here. This is the problem of *fictionalised* texts, even though there are clearly autobiographical elements in them. I acknowledge that

my reading has the consequence of underplaying at times the complicity of these texts with unhealthy social attitudes towards PWAs and homosexuals. I would point out that there is no intention on my part to downplay such attitudes which were in part responsible for the disastrous approach to prevention work that France adopted in the mid- to late 1980s.

4 Testimony, Self-Avowal and Confession

1 B. Paillard, *L'Epidémie: carnets d'un sociologue*, Paris, Stock, 1994; J.-L. Maxence, *Les Écrivains sacrifiées des années Sida*, Paris, Bayard, 1995; Frédéric Martel, *Le Rose et le noir*, Paris, Seuil, 1996.

2 M. Simonin, *Danger de vie*, Paris, Séguier, 1986. Page references to *Danger de vie* are placed within parentheses. The title constitutes a pun on 'Danger de mort' ('Danger of death') and these are also the last words of the book.

3 It was Professor Rozenbaum who finally informed me in a letter (30 April 1997), 'Monsieur Simonin alas died in December 1987 after deciding voluntarily to interrupt his medical follow-up.'

4 It is regrettable that following a restructuring of *Libération*, the archives have been closed to researchers and are available only to journalists, so I have not been able to study Simonin's letters in this newspaper.

5 'Aujourd'hui la vie': 'L'homosexualité', Antenne 2, 28 May 1982 (Simonin appeared in person); 'Le Magazine', Antenne 2, 10 October 1985 (his contribution was dropped); 'Au nom de l'amour', Fr3, 11 December 1985 (appeared anonymously); 'Les dossiers de l'écran': 'Le sida ou la peste du XXème siècle', Antenne 2, 4 March 1986 (appeared in person); 'Médecine à la Une: Le sida', TF1, 16 December 1986 (appeared in person).

6 The ACT-UP collective denounces the univocal image of HIV-positive people projected by these three writers: ACT-UP Paris, *Le Sida*, p. 368. Murray Pratt considers these arguments and brings new light to bear on the issue in 'A Walk Along the Side of the Motorway: AIDS and the Spectacular Body of Hervé Guibert', in O. Heathcote, A. Hughes and James S. Williams, eds, *Gay Signatures*, London, Berg, 1998, pp. 151–72.

7 ACT-UP Paris, *Le Sida*, pp. 176–77.

8 For an ideological analysis of the choice of the 'confession' genre, see the conclusion to Chapter 2 on Juliette.

9 M. Pratt, *Viral Discourse, Virtual Identity: National Sexuality and Cultures of AIDS in France*, London, Continuum, 2002, forthcoming.

10 Wendy Hollway, 'Gender Difference and the Production of Subjectivity', in Henriques et al., *Changing the Subject*, p. 226.

11 The politics of visibility of the 1970s led by Hocquenghem had started to have an impact, and a younger generation was now 'coming out' in the early 1980s.

12 'Inside Out', in Fuss, ed., *Inside/Out*, pp. 1–10 (p. 4).

13 J. Robert-Grandpierre and A. Zulian, 'Nouvelles Donnes', in B. Pralong,

J. Robert-Grandpierre and A. Zulian, *Sida, Paroles intimes et nouvelles donnes*, Geneva, Éditions IES, Annales du Centre de Recherche Sociale, No. 30, 1992, p. 69.

14 Lévy and Nouss, 'La Violence dans la fiction romanesque sur le Sida', p. 131.

15 The irony of fate being that it was no doubt Dr Rozenbaum who was contacted by the journalists who wanted an HIV-positive person who was willing to appear openly (because it is known that he was monitoring the progress of both Simonin and the professor).

16 The use of the masculine 'tous' here shows clearly that at the time AIDS was above all associated with men. The name of the witness in question is not given in the television programme, hence he will have to remain anonymous.

17 Michael Pollack, *Les Homosexuels et le sida: Sociologie d'une épidémie*, Paris, Éditions A. M. Métailié, 1988, p. 106. Pollack calls Simonin 'R.' in his book.

18 Pollack, *Les Homosexuels et le sida*, p. 108.

19 Pollack, *Les Homosexuels et le sida*, p. 104.

20 Thomé-Renault, *Le Traumatisme de la mort annoncée*, p. 62.

21 Thomé-Renault, *Le Traumatisme de la mort annoncée*, p. 62.

22 Thomé-Renault, *Le Traumatisme de la mort annoncée*, p. 63.

23 Judith Butler discusses the difficulties of grieving when the grief remains unspeakable in the context of homosexual love and loss. See Butler, 'Melancholy Gender / Refused Identification', pp. 21–36. See also Lorraine Sherr, ed., *Grief and AIDS*, New York, Wiley and Son, 1995.

24 G. Kaufman, *The Psychology of Shame*, London, Routledge, 1989, p. 49.

25 Lévy and Nouss, 'La Violence dans la fiction romanesque sur le Sida', p. 137.

26 C. Bourdin, *Le Fil*, Paris, La Différence, 1994.

27 H. Guibert, *Le Protocole compassionnel*, Paris, Gallimard, 1991.

28 My thanks go to David Jackson and Annabell who suggested readings having a direct bearing on what I was trying to express, and to Murray Pratt and Mireille Rosello for their comments on my first draft.

29 Wetsel, 'The Best of Times, the Worst of Times', p. 103. Elisabeth Schemla, 'Mon sida par Jean-Paul Aron', interview, *Le Nouvel Observateur*, 30 octobre–5 novembre 1987, pp. 126–31.

30 For instance, Grmek, 'Un historien face à la littérature du sida', p. 36, claims that Aron carved a path for a writer like Guibert. See also Danthe, 'Le sida et les lettres', p. 54; Marsan, *La Vie blessée*, p. 233; Boullant, 'Latex, mensonges et melo', p. 53.

31 Jean-Paul Aron, *Les Modernes*, Paris, Gallimard, 1984.

32 Jean-Paul Aron, *Mon sida*, Paris, Christian Bourgois Éditeur, 1988. Page references are inserted in the text in brackets. *Mon sida* was revised by Aron from the original interview (p. 6) but there are very few textual modifications, most changes being stylistic. One significant change is that in the interview Aron says that it was at his own request that his brother arranged for him to be tested for the HIV virus (p. 129), while in the book he states that he was tested because of his brother's insistence (p. 17).

33 For an excellent analysis of all these instances, see Danthe, 'Le sida et les lettres', especially the section 'Nommer ou non la maladie', pp. 54–56.

34 Harvey, 'Sidaïques/sidéens', p. 325.

35 Foucault, *The History of Sexuality*, Volumes 1 and 2.

36 For instance, Marty-Lavauzelle, 'Chronique d'une mort annoncée', p. 72.

37 Jean-Paul Aron and Roger Kempf, *Le Pénis et la démoralisation de l'Occident*, Paris, Grasset, 1978.

38 See, for instance, references to Weeks's two books in the introduction.

39 Lévy and Nouss, *Sida-Fiction*, p. 199.

40 Henriques et al., *Changing the Subject*, p. 260.

41 Edelman, 'The Plague of Discourse', p. 315.

42 'Sida: après l'aveu' ('AIDS: after the confession'), Antenne 2, 21 June 1988, with Daniel Costelle and Elisabeth Schemla.

43 Marsan, *La Vie blessée*, p. 235.

44 Marsan, *La Vie blessée*, p. 235.

45 For further reading, see Rommel Mendès-Leite, *Le Sens de l'Altérité, Penser les (homo)sexualités*, Paris, L'Harmattan, 2000.

46 Marsan, *La Vie blessée*, p. 236.

5 Dreuilhe: Metaphor/Phantasy and Mobilisation

1 Alain Emmanuel Dreuilhe, *Corps à Corps, Journal de Sida*, Paris, Gallimard, 1987. References to this book are inserted in brackets in the body of the text. Dreuilhe had already published a dictionary and a book, *La société invertie*, Paris, Flammarion, 1979.

   Danthe makes the point that by calling his book 'Journal de Sida' rather than 'Journal *du* Sida', Dreuilhe could be echoing 'Journal de guerre' ('War journal') (more often than not this subtlety is lost on commentators who write 'Journal *du* Sida'). Danthe, 'Le sida et les lettres', p. 60.

2 This description is in line with Winer's, where the virus is described as an enemy who, thanks to its disguise, tricks the border police (the T4 cells) and invades our territory. Writing in the 1990s, Guibert uses the analogy of the computer game, the Pacman. Guibert, *À l'ami qui ne m'a pas sauvé la vie*, p. 13.

3 Examples: 'La tentation de déserter; Le front et l'arrière; Le Liban de mon corps' ('The Temptation of Desertion; The War Zone and the Home Front; My Body, My Beirut'). All translations are from *Mortal Embrace: Living with AIDS*, trans. Linda Coverdale, New York, Hill and Wang, 1988. Where I have felt the need to change the translation, this is indicated by the fact that there is a direct quotation of the text in English but I have not provided a page number to the English edition of the book.

4 More curiously Alain Emmanuel Dreuilhe becomes Emmanuel Dreuilhe. There is also an additional epigraph by Marguerite Yourcenar in which she compares illness to war.

5 I shall use Dreuilhe as shorthand when referring to the narrator and the author but the points I made in the introduction about author/narrator, truth/fiction still apply here.

6 In the book Dreuilhe also talks about being married to Kristine Dreuilhe, who has been his companion for ten years (p. 156).

7 Dreuilhe talked about his book on French national television on a literary programme, 'Apostrophes', in the autumn of 1987. In it he claims that at first his journal was not destined for publication but only for personal use. The programme was entitled 'Les grandes épidémies: choléra, peste, sida' ('The great epidemics: cholera, plague and AIDS').

The similarity of approach to that of the narrator of *À l'ami qui ne m'a pas sauvé la vie* is striking. Guibert, *À l'ami qui ne m'a pas sauvé la vie*, p. 12.

8 This is remarkably close to Simonin's writing considered in Chapter 4: 'Pour moi, le virus qui me squatte est moins dangereux que l'isolement auquel on voudrait me condamner.' ('For me, the virus squatting in me is less dangerous than the isolation they would like to condemn me to.'); Simonin, *Danger de vie*, p. 240.

9 Danthe, 'Le sida et les lettres', p. 62.

10 In France, conscription for young men was compulsory and has only recently been abolished.

11 As we saw, Aron also uses a possessive pronoun 'Mon sida'.

12 The whole dynamic is reminiscent of Freud's biological mysticism of Eros and Thanatos.

13 Wetsel, 'The Best of Times, the Worst of Times', p. 100. On page 210, note 14, Wetsel cites the comparison made by Dreuilhe between the pleasure he takes in discussing his doctors and Saint-Loup's obsession with the Prince de Borodino in Proust's *À la recherche du temps perdu*. The reference to Dreuilhe (not given) is actually on pp. 60–61. There is also a parody of Proust's title in one of the sections called 'À la recherche de l'allié perdu' (pp. 55–65). Unfortunately, this is lost in the English translation since the play on words becomes 'Hope recaptured'. Dreuilhe had written his doctoral thesis on 'Proust and nationalisms' and he knew the work of Proust inside out. The title of his thesis also indicates that he had an early interest in nationalism, having previously studied in Paris at the prestigious Institut d'études politiques.

14 Dreuilhe talks about writing 'fragments d'un discours belliqueux' (p. 14) ('fragments of a warrior's discourse', p. 6), which echoes Roland Barthes's, *Fragments d'un discours amoureux*, Paris, Seuil, 1977.

15 'Kotler, mon spécialiste des intestins, […] m'a dit qu'il fallait serrer les dents (et les fesses, je présume)' (p. 61) ('Kotler, my gastrointestinal specialist, […] told me I had to clench my teeth (and my buttocks, I suppose)', p. 44).

16 On the model of 'Un seul être vous manque et tout est dépeuplé' (Lamartine, 'L'isolement', *Méditations poétiques*, I, 1820), he writes, 'J'ai repeuplé mon univers du seul être qui me manquât' (p. 60) ('I repopulated my universe with the only being whom I truly missed', p. 43). The being in question is AIDS.

17 After a rather lyrical passage, we read, 'Morceau de bravoure kitsch que tous les

discours patriotiques doivent comporter en forme de péroraison' (p. 190) ('A piece of bravura kitsch that every patriotic speech must include as part of its conclusion', p. 150).

18 Again, this is in line with Guibert's *À l'ami qui ne m'a pas sauvé la vie*, p. 111.

19 The parallel with Guibert is too striking not to be mentioned. Writing about the death of Muzil (whose character is based on Michel Foucault), the narrator writes that it is not so much Muzil's as his own death that he is writing about. See Boulé, *Hervé Guibert: Voices of the Self*, especially pp. 191–206.

20 'Alain-Emmanuel Dreuilhe: Un combat global', interview by Chantal Saint-Jarre, *Nuit Blanche*, Vol. 32, Part 6–7, 1988, pp. 54–57 (p. 56).

21 Graham Dawson, *Soldier Heroes: British Adventure, Empire and the Imagining of Masculinities*, London, Routledge, 1994.

22 Dawson, *Soldier Heroes*, p. 33.

23 Dawson, *Soldier Heroes*, p. 51.

24 Dawson, *Soldier Heroes*, p. 35.

25 Dreuilhe uses 'sidatique' throughout, explaining during 'Apostrophes' that living in the United States and not reading the French press, he was not sure which adjective to use. In France 'sidaïque' was controversial because it recalls 'judaïque', and the far right in France had made political use of their similarity to suggest that PWAs should be sent, not to concentration camps, but to sidatoria, a word that recalls crematoria, and that they should be tattooed (also reported by Dreuilhe, p. 165). The term 'sidéen' was officially endorsed in France by the Commission générale de terminologie in December 1987.

26 Dawson, *Soldier Heroes*, p. 47.

27 Chambers, *Facing It*, p. 28.

28 This is remarkably similar to what Simonin suffers in France as we saw in Chapter 4.

29 Susan Sontag, *AIDS and its Metaphors*, London, Penguin Books, 1988, pp. 94–95.

30 D.A Miller, 'Sontag's Urbanity', in Henry Abelove, Michèle Aina Barale and David M. Halperin, eds, *The Lesbian and Gay Studies Reader*, New York, Routledge, 1993, p. 219.

31 Miller, 'Sontag's Urbanity', p. 219.

32 Christophe Broqua, 'De quelques expressions collectives de la mémoire face au sida', *Ethnologie française*, XXVIII, No. 1, January–March 1998, p. 108.

33 Dawson, *Soldier Heroes*, p. 33.

34 Dawson, *Soldier Heroes*, p. 34.

35 Michael S. Sherry, 'The Language of War in AIDS Discourse', in Murphy and Poirier, eds, *Writing AIDS*, pp. 39, 50.

36 Sherry, 'The Language of War in AIDS Discourse', p. 45.

37 For instance, pp. 142, 163, 174, 180.

38 Saint-Jarre, 'Alain-Emmanuel Dreuilhe: Un combat global', p. 54.

39 Wetsel, 'The Best of Times, the Worst of Times', pp. 210–11.

40 This message is reinforced on the front cover of the French edition which features

a detail from Giorgio de Chirico, *Lion et gladiateurs* (1927) showing two gladiators fighting with a lion (presumably representing AIDS). One of the two gladiators is lying on the arena floor and appears to be mortally wounded while the other one is still fighting the lion who is about to devour the dying man.

41 Fritz Zorn, *Mars*, Munich, Kindler Verlag GmbH, 1977; French translation Paris, Gallimard, 1977.

42 Martine Delvaux, 'Des corps et des frontières: les lieux du sida', *L'Esprit créateur*, Vol. XXXVII, No. 3, Fall 1997, p. 88.

43 Delvaux, 'Des corps et des frontières', p. 88.

44 Dawson, *Soldier Heroes*, p. 48.

45 Lévy and Nouss, *Sida-Fiction*, pp. 174–75.

46 Dawson, *Soldier Heroes*, p. 48.

47 I had originally used 'fictional', but Ross Chambers pointed to the difference between the 'fictional' and the 'figural'. The latter shows that Dreuilhe's phantasy has a *symbolic* function: it solves for him a problem that cannot be solved in the real world, i.e., historically, and that recourse to the imaginary (the fictional) would not affect. Chambers believes that most of the discussion about metaphor is disqualified by the assumption that metaphor is a representation and that hence there are good and bad metaphors when in fact it is not a representation but a figuration; it does not signify by referring to an object but by providing an occasion for reading/interpretation, one whose 'object' is indistinguishable from the interpretation.

48 Dreuilhe knows that the Reagan administration had completely ignored the rising AIDS epidemic until finally convinced that it was not simply a 'gay plague' but was also affecting the heterosexual population (and not before thousands of Americans had died). Dreuilhe makes an interesting comparison between Reagan and Pétain, the head of the Vichy government, both washing their hands of the conflict (pp. 163–64).

49 Dawson, *Soldier Heroes*, p. 34.

50 Dawson, *Soldier Heroes*, p. 34.

51 Dawson, *Soldier Heroes*, p. 34.

52 This five-line paragraph is cut down to one short sentence in the English translation (p. 137).

53 To point to further similarities with Guibert, 'Quand je n'écris plus, je me meurs' ('When I no longer write, I wither and die'); Hervé Guibert, *Le Paradis*, Paris, Gallimard, 1992, p. 130.

54 There are many similarities in this respect with Simonin and his own loss of subjectivity through lack of sex; see Chapter 4.

55 For a study of writing as opposed to suicide, see Chambers, *Facing It*, especially 'Dying as an author', pp. 17–33.

Conclusion

1 Williamson, 'Every Virus Tells a Story', p. 70.
2 Williamson, 'Every Virus Tells a Story', p. 80.
3 Henriques et al., *Changing the Subject*, p. 220.
4 Jaccomard also believes that the French political climate of 'la cohabitation' (the situation in which the French President is in political opposition to the majority in the National Assembly), prevalent at the time in France, had an impact on early AIDS writing in France. For an interesting angle on this, see Colin Davis and Elizabeth Fallaize, *French Fiction in the Mitterrand Years: Memory, Narrative, Desire*, Oxford Studies in Modern European Culture, Oxford, Oxford University Press, 2000.
5 Foucault, *The History of Sexuality*, Volumes 1 and 2.
6 Weedon, *Feminist Practice and Poststructuralist Theory*, p. 120.
7 See Jaccomard, 'Du sexisme dans les écrits du sida', pp. 321–35.
8 Weedon, *Feminist Practice and Poststructuralist Theory*, p. 96.
9 This argument was first put to me by Ross Chambers.
10 Dreuilhe's book was written while he was living in the United States, but a similar sense of isolation colours his writing.
11 I owe this comparison to a discussion with Ross Chambers.
12 To date, the latest book concerning AIDS to be published in France is *L'Insecte* by Jean-Michel Iribarren in the series 'Solo', Paris, Seuil, 2000. In the book, the HIV virus is the main narrator, and tells the story of 'Tête perdue' ('Lost head') who died of an AIDS-related illness and of his partner 'Sang Inquiet' ('Worried blood') whom it has never managed to contaminate.
13 Dreuilhe, *Corps à corps*, p. 123.

Bibliography

Primary Texts

Aron, Jean-Paul, 'Mon sida', interview in *Le Nouvel Observateur*, 30 October–
   5 November 1987, by Elisabeth Schemla. Edition revised by J.-P. Aron,
   Mon sida, Paris, Christian Bourgois, 1988.
Dreuilhe, Alain Emmanuel, *Corps à Corps, Journal de Sida*, Paris, Gallimard,
   'Au vif du Sujet' series, 1987. Translated into English as *Mortal Embrace:
   Living with AIDS*, trans. Linda Coverdale, New York, Hill and Wang, 1988.
Juliette, *Pourquoi moi? Confession d'une jeune femme d'aujourd'hui*, Paris,
   Robert Laffont, 1987.
Laygues, Hélène, *Sida, Témoignage sur la vie et la mort de Martin*, Paris,
   Hachette, 1985.
Simonin, Michel, *Danger de vie*, Paris, Librairie Séguier, 1986.
Winer, Mike, *Bienvenue dans le monde du sida!*, Monaco, Le Rocher, 1988.

Other AIDS texts published in France in the 1980s

Belloc, David, *Képas*, Paris, Lieu Commun, 1989.
Chapsal, Madeleine, *Adieu l'amour*, Paris, Fayard, 1987.
Collard, Cyril, *Les Nuits fauves*, Paris, Flammarion, 1989.

Copi, *Une Visite inopportune*, Paris, Christian Bourgois, 1989.

Detrez, Conrad, *La Mélancolie du voyeur*, Paris, Denoël, 1986.

Fernandez, Dominique, *La Gloire du paria*, Paris, Grasset, 1987.

Hocquenghem, Guy, *Ève*, Paris, Albin Michel 1987.

Luria, Valéry [pseudonym of pianist Valéry Afanassiev], *La Chute de Babylone*, Paris, Belfont, 1985.

Matzneff, Gabriel, *Harrison Plaza*, Paris, La Table Ronde, 1988.

Mellis, Yves de, *Un Mal qui répand la Terreur*, Paris, Barré et Dayez, 1988.

Navarre, Yves, *Hôtel Styx*, Paris, Albin Michel, 1989.

Secondary Bibliography

'Alain-Emmanuel Dreuilhe: Un combat global', interview by Chantal Saint-Jarre, *Nuit Blanche*, Vol. 32, Part 6–7, 1988, pp. 54–57.

Abbott, Franklin, ed., *Men and Intimacy*, San Francisco, The Crossing Press Freedom, 1990.

Abelove, Henry, Michèle Aina Barale and David M. Halperin, eds, *The Lesbian and Gay Studies Reader*, New York, Routledge, 1993.

ACT-UP Paris, *Le Sida, Combien de divisions?*, Paris, Dagorno, 1994.

Agar, James, 'Writing the "Histoire" of AIDS in France', *French Cultural Studies*, Vol. 9, Part 3, No. 27, October 1998, pp. 411–18.

Angvik, Birger, 'Textual Constellations: AIDS and the Love of Writing in the Postmodern Era', *Journal of Latin American Cultural Studies*, Vol. 7, No. 2, 1998, pp. 165–83.

Apter, Emily, 'Fantom Images: Hervé Guibert and the Writing of "sida" in France', in Timothy F. Murphy and Suzanne Poirier, eds, *Writing AIDS: Gay Literature, Language and Analysis*, New York, Columbia University Press, 1993, pp. 83–97.

Arnal, Frank, *Résister ou disparaître: les homosexuels face au sida: la prévention de 1982 à 1992*, Paris, L'Harmattan, 1993.

Aron, Jean-Paul, *Les Modernes*, Paris, Gallimard, 1984.

Aron, Jean-Paul and Roger Kempf, *Le Pénis et la démoralisation de l'Occident*, Paris, Grasset, 1978.

Attridge, Derek, ed., *Acts of Literature*, London, Routledge, 1992.

Barthes, Roland, *Image, Music, Text*, New York, Hill and Wang, 1977.

Benjamin, Jessica, *The Bonds of Love: Psychoanalysis, feminism and the problem of domination*, London, Virago, 1990.

Berger, Maurice, Brian Wallis and Simon Watson, eds, *Constructing Masculinity*, London, Routledge, 1995.

Bersani, Leo, 'Is the Rectum a Grave?', in Douglas Crimp, ed., *AIDS: Cultural Analysis, Cultural Activism*, Cambridge, MA, MIT Press, 1988, pp. 197–222.

Boulé, Jean-Pierre, 'Hervé Guibert ou la radicalisation du projet sartrien d'écriture existentielle', in Ralph Sarkonak, ed., *Le Corps textuel d'Hervé Guibert*, Paris, Minard, 1997, pp. 25–42.

Boulé, Jean-Pierre, *Hervé Guibert: Voices of the Self*, Liverpool, Liverpool University Press, 1999. Published in France as *Hervé Guibert: L'entreprise de l'écriture du moi*, Paris, L'Harmattan, 2001.

Boulé, Jean-Pierre, 'Tout ange est terrible (À propos des articles nécrologiques sur Hervé Guibert)', *L'Esprit créateur*, Vol. XXXVII, No. 3, Fall 1997, pp. 61–71.

Boullant, François, 'Latex, mensonges et mélo… Sida et littérature', *Actes*, Nos. 71–72, 1990, pp. 50–58.

Bourdieu, Pierre, *La Domination masculine*, Paris, Seuil, 1998.

Brittan, Arthur, *Masculinity and Power*, Oxford, Blackwell, 1989.

Broqua, Christophe, 'De quelques expressions collectives de la mémoire face au sida', *Ethnologie française*, XXVIII, No. 1, January–March 1998, pp. 103–11.

Brunet, Jean-Baptiste, 'Tirer sérieusement des leçons', interview by J. C. Cauchy and J. Y. Le Talec, *Gai Pied Hebdo*, 24 October 1991.

Bulletin de Thanatologie, 27ème année, No. 95–96, November 1993, special issue 'Vivre le Sida'.

Butler, Judith, *Bodies That Matter*, New York, Routledge, 1993.

Butler, Judith, *Gender Trouble: Feminism and the Subversion of Identity*, New York, Routledge, 1990.

Butler, Judith, 'Melancholy Gender/Refused Identification', in Maurice Berger, Brian Wallis and Simon Watson, eds, *Constructing Masculinity*, London, Routledge, 1995, pp. 21–36.

Caron, David, *AIDS in French Culture: Social Ills, Literary Cures*, Madison, WI, University of Wisconsin Press, 2001.

Caron, David, '*Liberté, Égalité, Séropositivité*: AIDS, the French Republic, and the Question of Community', *French Cultural Studies*, Vol. 9, Part 3, No. 27, October 1998, pp. 281–93.

Carter, Erica and Simon Watney, eds, *Taking Liberties, AIDS and Cultural Politics*, London, Serpent's Tail, 1989.

Chambers, Ross, 'AIDS and the Culture of Accompaniment in France', *French Cultural Studies*, Vol. 9, Part 3, No. 27, October 1998, pp. 399–409.

Chambers, Ross, *Facing It, AIDS Diaries and the Death of the Author*, Ann

Arbor, MI, University of Michigan Press, 1998.

Chambers, Ross, 'The suicide experiment: Hervé Guibert's AIDS video, *La Pudeur ou l'impudeur*', *L'Esprit créateur*, Vol. XXXVII, No. 3, Fall 1997, pp. 72–82.

Chambers, Ross, 'Visitations: Operatic quotations in three AIDS films', *UTS Review*, Vol. 2, No. 2, November 1996, pp. 24–67.

Connell, R.W., *Masculinities*, Oxford, Polity Press, 1995.

Coria, C., *El Sexo Oculto del Dinero*, Buenos Aires, Grupo Editor Latino-americano, Coleccion Controversia, 1986.

Crimp, Douglas, ed., *AIDS: Cultural Analysis, Cultural Activism*, Cambridge, MA, MIT Press, 1988.

Danthe, Michel, 'Le sida et les lettres: un bilan francophone', *Équinoxe*, No. 5, Spring 1991, pp. 51–85.

Davis, Colin, and Elizabeth Fallaize, *French Fiction in the Mitterrand Years: Memory, Narrative, Desire*, Oxford Studies in Modern European Culture, Oxford, Oxford University Press, 2000.

Dawson, Graham, *Soldier Heroes: British Adventure, Empire and the Imagining of Masculinities*, London, Routledge, 1994.

Delvaux, Martine, 'Des corps et des frontières: les lieux du sida', *L'Esprit créateur*, Vol. XXXVII, No. 3, Fall 1997, pp. 83–93.

Derrida, Jacques, 'The Law of Genre', in Derek Attridge, ed., *Acts of Literature*, London, Routledge, 1992, pp. 221–52.

Dewey, Joseph, 'Music for a Closing: Responses to AIDS in Three American Novels', in Emmanuel S. Nelson, ed., *AIDS: The Literary Response*, New York, Twayne Publishers, 1992, pp. 23–38.

Dollimore, Jonathan, *Sexual Dissidence. Augustine to Wilde, Freud to Foucault*, Oxford, Clarendon Press, 1991.

Dowsett, G.W., *Practising Desire, Homosexual sex in the era of AIDS*, Stanford, CA, Stanford University Press, 1996.

Edelman, Lee, *Homographesis*, London, Routledge, 1994.

Edelman, Lee, 'The Plague of Discourse: Politics, Literary Theory, and AIDS', *South Atlantic Quarterly*, Vol. 88, No. 1, Winter 1989, pp. 43–64.

Équinoxe, No. 5, Spring 1991, 'Le sida et les lettres', special issue edited by Michel Danthe and François Wasserfallen.

Éribon, Didier, *Les Études gay et lesbiennes*, Paris, Centre Georges Pompidou, 1998.

Ethnologie française, XXVIII, No. 1 'Sida: deuil, mémoire, nouveaux rituels', January–March 1998.

Foucault, Michel, *The History of Sexuality, Volume 1, The Will to Knowledge*,

Harmondsworth, Penguin, 1981; *The History of Sexuality, Volume 2, The Use of Pleasure*, Harmondsworth, Viking, 1986.

Foucault, Michel, *Language, Counter-Memory, Practice*, Ithaca, NY, Cornell University Press, 1977.

Freadman, Anne, and Amanda Macdonald, *What is this thing called 'genre'?*, Mount Nebo, Queensland, Boombana Publications, 1992.

Freeman, Mark, *Rewriting the Self: History, Memory, Narrative*, London, Routledge, 1993.

French Cultural Studies, Vol. 9, Part 3, No. 27, October 1998, special issue 'AIDS in France', guest editors Jean-Pierre Boulé and Murray Pratt.

Frogier, Larys, 'Homosexuals, and the AIDS Crisis in France', in Joshua Oppenheimer and Helena Reckitt, eds, *Acting on AIDS: Sex, Drugs and Politics*, London, Serpent's Tail, 1997, pp. 346–59.

Fuss, Diana, ed., *Inside/Out: Lesbian Theories, Gay Theories*, New York, Routledge, 1991.

Grmek, Mirko, 'Un historien face à la littérature du sida', *Équinoxe*, No. 5, Spring 1991, pp. 33–40.

Guibert, Hervé, *À l'ami qui ne m'a pas sauvé la vie*, Paris, Gallimard, 1990. Translated by Linda Coverdale, *To the Friend Who Did Not Save My Life*, London, Quartet Books, 1991.

Guibert, Hervé, *Le Paradis*, Paris, Gallimard, 1992.

Guntrip, Harry, *Psychoanalytic Theory, Therapy and the Self*, London, Karnac Books, 1977; original edition The Hogarth Press, 1971.

Hargreaves, Alec, *Immigration, 'Race' and Ethnicity in Contemporary France*, London, Routledge, 1995.

Harvey, Robert, 'Sidaïques/sidéens: French Discourses on AIDS', *Contemporary French Civilization*, Vol. 16, No. 192, Summer/Fall 1992, pp. 308–35.

Hearn, Jeff, *The Gender of Oppression*, Brighton, Wheatsheaf Books, 1987.

Heathcote, Owen, Alex Hughes and James S. Williams, eds, *Gay Signatures*, London, Berg, 1998.

Henriques, Julian, Wendy Hollway, Cathy Urwin, Couze Venn and Valerie Walkerdine, *Changing the Subject: Psychology, social regulation and subjectivity*, London, Methuen, 1984.

Hocquenghem, Guy, *Le Désir homosexuel*, Paris, Éditions universitaires, 1972.

Hollway, Wendy, 'Gender Difference and the Production of Subjectivity', in Julian Henriques, Wendy Hollway, Cathy Urwin, Couze Venn and Valerie Walkerdine, *Changing the Subject: Psychology, social regulation and subjectivity*, London, Methuen, 1984, pp. 227–63.

Jaccomard, Hélène, 'Du sexisme dans les écrits du sida', *French Cultural Studies*, Vol. 9, Part 3, No. 27, October 1998, pp. 321–35.

Jelinek, E., *Women's Autobiography*, Bloomington, IN, Indiana University Press, 1980.

Kaufman, G., *The Psychology of Shame*, London, Routledge, 1989.

Kimmel, Michael S., and Martin P. Levine, 'Men and *AIDS*', in Franklin Abbott, ed., *Men and Intimacy*, San Francisco, The Crossing Press Freedom, 1990, pp. 90–102.

Kramer, Larry, *The Normal Heart*, New York, Plume, 1985.

L'Esprit créateur, Vol. XXXVII, No. 3, Fall 1997, special issue on 'The Politics and Aesthetics of Contamination and Purity', guest editor Mireille Rosello.

Lévy, Joseph and Alexis Nouss, *Sida-Fiction, Essai d'anthropologie romanesque*, Lyon, Presses universitaires de Lyon, 1994.

Lévy, Joseph and Alexis Nouss, 'La Violence dans la fiction romanesque sur le Sida', *Bulletin de Thanatologie*, No. 95–96, November 1993, pp. 115–44.

Marsan, Hugo, 'Le roman du sida', *Gai Pied Hebdo*, No. 451, 3 January 1991, p. 20.

Marsan, Hugo, *La Vie blessée*, Paris, Maren Sell, 1989.

Marshall, Bill, *Guy Hocquenghem: Theorising the Gay Nation*, London, Pluto Press, 1996.

Martel, Frédéric, *Le Rose et le noir, Les homosexuels en France depuis 1968*, Paris, Seuil, 1996. Translated into English by Jane Marie Todd as *The Pink and the Black: Homosexuals in France since 1968*, Stanford, CA, Stanford University Press, 2000.

Marty-Lavauzelle, Arnaud, 'Chronique d'une mort annoncée', *Bulletin de Thanatologie*, No. 95–96, November 1993, pp. 71–78.

Maxence, Jean-Luc, *Les Écrivains sacrifiés des années Sida*, Paris, Bayard Éditions, 1995.

Mendès-Leite, Rommel, *Le Sens de l'Altérité, Penser les (homo)sexualités*, Paris, L'Harmattan, 2000.

Miller, D.A, 'Sontag's Urbanity', in Henry Abelove, Michèle Aina Barale and David M. Halperin, eds, *The Lesbian and Gay Studies Reader*, New York, Routledge, 1993, pp. 212–20.

Mitchell, J., and J. Rose, eds, *Feminine Sexuality*, London, Macmillan, 1982.

Mitchell, Juliet, ed., *The Selected Melanie Klein*, London, Penguin Books, 1991.

Morrison, James, 'The Repression of the Returned: AIDS and Allegory', in Emmanuel S. Nelson, ed., *AIDS: The Literary Response*, New York, Twayne Publishers, 1992, pp. 167–74.

Murphy, Timothy F., 'Testimony', in Timothy F. Murphy and Suzanne Poirier, eds, *Writing AIDS: Gay Literature, Language and Analysis*, New York, Columbia University Press, 1993, pp. 306–20.

Murphy, Timothy F. and Suzanne Poirier, eds, *Writing AIDS: Gay Literature, Language and Analysis*, New York, Columbia University Press, 1993.

Nelson, Emmanuel S., ed., *AIDS: The Literary Response*, New York, Twayne Publishers, 1992.

Oppenheimer, Joshua and Helena Reckitt, *Acting on AIDS: Sex, Drugs and Politics*, London, Serpent's Tail, 1997.

Paillard, Bernard, *L'Épidémie: carnets d'un sociologue*, Paris, Stock, 1994.

Pastore, Judith Laurence, ed., *Confronting AIDS through Literature*, Chicago, University of Illinois Press, 1993.

Pastore, Judith Laurence, 'Suburban AIDS: Alice Hoffman's *At Risk*', in Emmanuel S. Nelson, ed., *AIDS: The Literary Response*, New York, Twayne Publishers, 1992, pp. 39–49.

Pauwels, Louis, 'Le monôme des zombies', *Figaro Magazine*, 6 December 1986.

Pollack, Michael, *Les Homosexuels et le sida. Sociologie d'une épidémie*, Paris, Éditions A.M. Métailié, 1988.

Pralong, B., J. Robert-Grandpierre and A. Zulian, *Sida, Paroles intimes et nouvelles donnes*, Geneva, Les éditions IES, Annales du Centre de Recherche Sociale No. 30, 1992.

Pratt, Murray, 'AIDS Prevention, Gay Identity and National Homophobia in France', in Joe Andrew, Malcolm Crook, Diana Holmes and Eva Kolinsky, eds, *Why Europe? Problems of Culture and Identity*, London, Macmillan, 2000, pp. 142–69.

Pratt, Murray, 'The defence of the straight state: heteronormativity, AIDS in France, and the space of the nation', *French Cultural Studies*, Vol. 9, Part 3, No. 27, October 1998, pp. 263–80.

Pratt, Murray, *Viral Discourse, Virtual Identity: National Sexuality and Cultures of AIDS in France*, London, Continuum, 2002.

Pratt, Murray, 'A Walk Along the Side of the Motorway: AIDS and the Spectacular Body of Hervé Guibert', in O. Heathcote, A. Hughes and James S. Williams, eds, *Gay Signatures*, London, Berg, 1998, pp. 151–72.

Redman, Peter, 'Invasion of the Monstrous Others: Heterosexual Masculinities, the "AIDS Carrier" and the Horror Genre', in D. L. Steinberg, D. Epstein and R. Johnson, eds, *Border Patrols*, London, Cassell, 1997, pp. 98–116.

Robert-Grandpierre, J., and A. Zulian, 'Nouvelles Donnes', in B. Pralong,

J. Robert-Grandpierre and A. Zulian, *Sida, Paroles intimes et nouvelles donnes*, Geneva, Éditions IES, Annales du Centre de Recherche Sociale, No. 30, 1992, pp. 51–112.

Sarkonak, Ralph, ed., *Le Corps textuel d'Hervé Guibert*, Paris, Minard, 'Écritures contemporaines' series, 1997.

Savigny, Jean de, *Le SIDA et les fragilités françaises: nos réactions face à l'épidémie*, Paris, Albin Michel, 1995.

Schehr, Lawrence R., 'Hervé Guibert under Bureaucratic Quarantine', *L'Esprit créateur*, Vol. XXXIV, No. 1, Spring 1994, pp. 73–82.

Segal, Lynne, *Slow Motion: Changing Masculinities, Changing Men*, London, Virago, 1990.

Setbon, Michel, *Pouvoirs contre sida*, Paris, Seuil, 1993.

Sherr, Lorraine, ed., *Grief and AIDS*, New York, Wiley and Son, 1995.

Sherry, Michael S., 'The Language of War in AIDS Discourse', in Timothy F. Murphy and Suzanne Poirier, eds, *Writing AIDS: Gay Literature, Language and Analysis*, New York, Columbia University Press, 1993, pp. 39–53.

Smith, Anna Marie, *New Right Discourse on Race and Sexuality: Britain 1968–1990*, Cambridge, Cambridge University Press, 1994.

Sontag, Susan, *AIDS and its Metaphors*, London, Penguin Books, 1988.

Souyris, Anne, 'L'épidémie au féminin', *Le Journal du sida*, No. 48, March 1993, 'Dossier Femmes', pp. 13–14.

Stallybrass, P. and A. White, *The Politics and Poetics of Transgression*, London, Methuen, 1986.

Staudacher, Carol, *Men and Grief*, San Francisco, New Harbinger Publications, 1991.

Steinberg D. L., D. Epstein and R. Johnson, eds, *Border Patrols*, London, Cassell, 1997.

Stone, Albert E., 'Autobiography and American Culture', *American Studies: An International Newsletter*, 12, Winter 1972.

Tabin, J. Kraut, *On the Way to Self*, New York, Columbia University Press, 1985.

Theweleit, Klaus, *Male Fantasies*, Cambridge, Polity Press, 1987. Originally published as *Männerphantasien*, Vol. 1, *Frauen, Fluten, Körper, Geschichte*, Verlag Roter Stern, 1977.

Thomé-Renault, Annette, *Le Traumatisme de la mort annoncée, Psychosomatique et Sida*, Paris, Dunod, 1995.

Walkerdine, Valerie, *Schoolgirl Fictions*, London, Verso, 1990.

Watney, Simon, *Policing Desire. Pornography, AIDS and the Media*, London, Methuen, 1987.

Watney, Simon, *Practices of Freedom: Selected Writings on HIV/AIDS*, London, River Oram Press, 1994.

Weedon, Chris, *Feminist Practice and Poststructuralist Theory*, Oxford, Blackwell, 1987.

Weeks, Jeffrey, *Sex, Politics and Society*, Harlow, Longman, 2nd edn, 1994.

Weeks, Jeffrey, *Sexuality and its Discontents*, London, Routledge, 1985.

Welldon, Estela V., *Mother, Madonna, Whore*, New York, The Guilford Press, 1988.

Wetsel, David, 'The Best of Times, the Worst of Times: The Emerging Literature of AIDS in France', in Emmanuel S. Nelson, ed., *AIDS: The Literary Response*, New York, Twayne Publishers, 1992, pp. 95–113.

Williamson, Judith, 'Every Virus Tells a Story. The Meanings of HIV and AIDS', in Erica Carter and Simon Watney, eds, *Taking Liberties, AIDS and Cultural Politics*, London, Serpent's Tail, 1989, pp. 69–80.

Woods, Gregory, 'La fin d'Arcadie: *Gai Pied* and the "cancer gai"', *French Cultural Studies*, Vol. 9, Part 3, No. 27, October 1998, pp. 295–305.

Index